Phil Stodds was brought up on a Pembrokeshire farm by a loving—if unconventional—family. Schooling was more about sports than books. After a semi-professional rugby career alongside building a successful business, he returned to his calling to be a farmer. This is where he began to write about his and others' life experiences in poems. Even though Phil is dyslexic, this does not hold him back. His life has, let's say, been very colourful and as his minister says, "Phil will go where angels fear to tread."

To all who shaped my life:

the knockers, the likers, the lovers.

Phil Stodds

POEMS FROM THE HEART

AUSTIN MACAULEY PUBLISHERS™

LONDON • CAMBRIDGE • NEW YORK • SHARJAH

A CIP catalogue record for this title is available from the British Library.

ISBN 9781528982238 (Paperback)
ISBN 9781528982245 (ePub e-book)

www.austinmacauley.com

First Published (2020)
Austin Macauley Publishers Ltd
25 Canada Square
Canary Wharf
London
E14 5LQ

Thanks to my family, especially my father, who shaped me from a wild colt into a good horse.

Introduction

I have written these poems from my everyday observations as a father, farmer and total nonconformist. My education was very basic; I learned more from a loving father on a farm than a book. I had the most loving mother and the most competitive brother, as well as a grounding sister. This book is not for someone who is looking for punctuation and perfect spelling. The poems you are about to read are brought about by tabulate periods in my life from a total high to beneath the rock at the bottom. Please enjoy.

*"Failure is not getting knocked down;
it is not getting back up again."*

My Path

I was bought up on a farm
Where I grew fast and strong in the arm
Hard work, red meat I took no harm
But life dealt our family a few bad hands
And forced us to make other plans
And from the farm we had to leave
So we closed the gate with no reprieve.
With worn out tools we journeyed on
pulling together everyone
Slowly moving forward never looking back
Learning to play a hand and knowing when to stack
No lane to protect you from them that fleece
The green fields that embraced you that gave you so such peace.
The street wise fellows that I did have to meet
Bare knuckles in a bar room…
…is how they liked to greet
Others take out a knife; want to cut and leave a scar;
This to a country boy all seemed so bizarre.
But what they had not bargained for…
Was this farmer boy was brought up tuff
By a father who taught him all the important stuff
To fight and toil in summer's heat
Chasing sheep in winter sleet
Cattle kicked and butted…he felt no pain
Long Days spent picking stones, hardening hands was not in vain
Digging ditches with pick and shovel
Lessons taught he would never grovel
Just working until work was done

Never grumbling; dad made it fun
Building character by the tonne
Shaping me for whets to come...
Challenges that may arise
Not only to use my arm to gain the prize;
But to think and stay calm
And if needed
Switch on a little charm.
As time went by and I did well
Now my business I could sell
Land and toil filled my head
Not put up my feet and more time in bed
Then that itch came back to stay
And god he worked in a mysterious way
The land and farming life that I had to leave
I now at last began to grieve
And as with every addiction:
Just a sip was all it took...
To get me back on the hook
So god did call me back again
To fields of peace and a protective lane
Life lessons he did teach...
and I did learn
That a farmer's life I did yearn
So this is where my path did lead
A country life is all I need.

A 'Man's Man'...

A 'man's man' you will see
…is full of grit not mutiny
Not a charlatan
Just full of guts, spirit and determination
He gets the job done and then moves on.
Here are but a few who did their task
Without an ask:
Gandhi who did not raise a fist must come first on this list
Ail with his fist and shuffle
But for all his waffle
Draft papers in the bin
Asian war not for him
Nelson with his one good eye
Beat the French and did die
Douglas Barder shot down in his plane
Lost his legs but flew again
But some a halo they could never wear;
Like Paddy Mayne of SAS and lion's fame…
Led from the front for him it was a game
For he did dare and he did win
Alas no V C…too much sin.
Even in our fiction they are there;
John Wayne whom I'm a fan
Always plays the 'Man's man'
Now the best I hope you agree
Is Tommy f…in Shelby?
Now he a wrong "un"
Bad man's man but somewhere in us we can find forgiveness
for his crimes
Cos he helped others in hard times

Even in song
They come along
Big bad John in his pit
Saved his men then bought it
For I've been called a 'Man's man'
By men for whom I'd go to war
Men that I've been taught
Men that I have fought
Men that I look up to
Men that are YOU
To sum it up
We must all agree and it must always be
A MAN'S MAN IS
                    YOU and ME.

Irena

Irena met by St. Peter at Heaven's gate
At the ripe old age of 98
It was in a Warsaw ghetto in time of war
Many years before
She got a job as a plumber
But she was not there for taps and shower.
In her tool box she did hide, babies of the Jewish kind
That those SS pigs couldn't find
In the back of her van she kept her dog and he could bark and bite
…and Hitler's bully boys on the gate would let her through without a fight
The children's name's she did write
…hidden in a jar buried out of sight
Over 2500 were saved this way
Then one day she was caught and had to pay
Both legs broken, arms as well…beaten half way to hell
But she did survive to dig up her jar;
Tried in vain to re-unite the kids with their kin to ease their pain
What an unforgiving task most mums and dads had been gassed
But she knew what to do: homed them to be loved again
…with folks who washed away their pain
Now Irena was not forgotten
And In 2007…
Just one year before she left for heaven
She was noble prize listed…
But overlooked to my surprise
It was Al Gore that took the prize!

So let's not forget that Warsaw plumber and her dog
That did not fear the SS hood while doing so much good
Saving as many as she could:
Irena Sendler.

Unknown Warrior
7/11/1920

"Dug him up from where he lay
Stretched out there in Christian clay."
He was number four
Three more brave dead lads had gone before
From blood stained fields where the poppies grow Ypres,
Arras, Asine and the Somme
All four here in a military row
With the union flag draped over them
Taken down special
From where they did once blow
Sentries posted while
Brigadier-General Wyatt and Colonel Gell
Chose the man to come home from where he fell
A French guard of honour watched over this unknown warrior
all though that cold November night
Now next day the 8th
And that brave lad was laid into an oak coffin
Face covered in the best of Irish linen
On top was placed a crusaders sword and shield inscribed
Unknown British warrior Great War 1914/18 for king and
country
They could I have said so much more
Like, thank you sorry so many of you brave lads where blown
to pieces in this man made hell called war
On the 9th another cold November day
Loaded on to a gun carriage and finally on his way
Tolling Bells and bugle calls and another French guard of
honour

Marechal Foche saluted him as they boarded him bound for
Dover
Aboard HMS Venom
His coffin stood on the deck covered in wreaths draped in the
Union Jack
For not long now brave lad you will soon be back
As they docked under the white cliffs years have passed
Though this Warrior
had not aged since he had seen them last
Nineteen guns sounded out saluting him
Normally only reserved for the highest ranks
I think he had heard too many guns and when they stopped he
gave thanks
Now he was home on British caulk
Not for him the hero's walk
Down that dockside into the arms of his loving mother or
picking up his son, wife or other
Not for him his life was ended far away
By bullets and bombs knee deep in blood and clay
At least he's home here today
And tomorrow at Westminster is where
He will finally lay
Resting his weary head in the tomb for so many dead
For he is only one soldiers but unknown
Other left to rot no grave do they fill
517,773 lost without a trace
But who's to say they are not them here in this final resting
place
In his grave so many families find so much hope
The idea of the unknown warrior was a Christian mans who
came home from that hell and struggled to cope
Padre David Railton was his name
Not that we can say we know of his fame
It was not for him the glory of war
But with humility to remember they who sacrificed so much
And more
And now it's for us to pick up his flag remembering other in
conflict and war

That keep us safe as enemies come banging on Britain's door
So folks you must see
That 11hour 11th November is so important I do hope
You agree.

11/11/11
Don't Forget It

Cambridge University you privileged protected pets
Really you voted to turn your backs on ours…and yes yours too…blown up vets
Not to mention our dead that still lay rotting in Flanders hallowed ground
Blown to bits so badly that nothing could be found
Next time you take you seats in your debating camber
I think you liberal yellow poshed up toffs best you start to remember…
… Sword, Omaha's
Juno and Gold
For these names of which you should never have to be told
Where young men younger than you showed the Nazis how to be bold
Who laid their lives for you again why should you have to be told
You are called our new elite
To those boys who died you couldn't hold a sheet
Some of you poisonous little snakes
After this little vote we know now you're a bunch of fucking fakes
In time you will try to run for office to be a leach
Feeding off our country and the memoirs of them on the beach
You privileged fuckers sitting in your dorms with your laptops in your hand
Think of all the lads rotting in the sand
Rowing in your boats up and down the Thames only pain you feel is them legs you have to shave

While you should be voting to remember them that gave it all
so brave
Think of their families that place that blood red poppy
On that white stone grave, Dam you all
May god have mercy on your sole?
Cos when you're gone you will want to be remembered when
you're laid in your deep dark hole.
Phil Stodds
15 /10/ 2018

Terrorist

Bomb makers be headers, plane crashers, lorry smashers
All for what? It's not for me
But then I think again
William Wallis believed his cause
When did good and evil become so perverse
We all think we're right
But don't show up with dynamite
Who's to say they are wrong
We have all marched with the throng
Bra burner, fox hunters, ban the bombs Greenham commoners
Coal miners stood their ground
With copper on horses all around
So tell me over a drink, was Robin Hood who we think?
With his men he stood for good in the trees in Sherwood
Law at that time king John who ran the show
Wanted robin and his men swinging from his rope to and fro
William Wallis what a legend he's become
Longshanks did not agree and slit his guts for all to see
So in time you may agree
The men with thoughts of anarchy and bloody fuelled killing spree
Will we turn our coats to them that don't always win the battle?
Not at the time when we should
But when we see the way they were misunderstood
So in time when trouble has past
Thoughts of what flag we should have and nailed to which mast
Why did we not listen to righteous ones?

That talked and stooped and tipped their hat
Lived by trust, deeds and their word
History shows neither side would ever listen
To that man who knows how to stop the blood that still flows
from men battling with either arrow from a bow
Or napalm with it death foul glow
Well now it's Time to put away the dynamite
Start to listen so children can sleep safe at night.

The Brotherhood

Around men I have been;
Some kind, some mean
But at the age of nineteen
I met a bunch the like I'd never seen
In early August 85
At Pill Park my rugby life came alive
For I thought that I was good
But not in the eyes of this brotherhood...
So I strutted up to this throng
From the off I'd got it wrong
These village boys had seen it all before
And let me tell you they laid down the law
Not in words for you to hear
"No" in blood and sweat and the odd tear
For this team I did join
Was built on honesty trust and a beer
They were, on their day, a team to fear...
But something else they all played for
Was not the win, the lose or draw
They were village boys that grew up together; a band of
brothers they knew the score
Here I was on their turf
A lone wolf on his back
Longing to join this pack
Slowly overtime their snarling stopped
...and me to this team they did adopt
Around these young men I grew
They bought my confidence through.
In that first year we did gel
But it could not throw off our losing spell

It was not about the score for these guys
They had made promises in their eyes
There was not quitter in this band
And so they took me in
Cos they knew I would always fight for the win
Next year came fast, new coach and he knew what to do;
A gentleman, he could fill any shoe
But don't be fooled he was tuff as teak a farmer too
He gave us discipline and a will to win
…beating the best Whitland, Narberth all done with my kin
For now they had let me in.
And for ever when I'm asked, "Who did you play for Stodds?"
I will claim:
Llangwm is where it began and finished
Among men with guts and grit who would never even think
to quit
I have played with others
…but these men will always be my band of brothers.

Sandy Haven

Sea trimmed trees swaying in autumns cooling breeze
Gulls gathering in shimmering stream
Boats marooned in muddy greenie sand
Weed knotted ropes
Tied by the seas calloused hand
Cackling rooks hide in turning leaves
All to sound of the sea wailing for her dying waves how she
do grieve
All made by God for them that believe

Caretaker

When god had rested on the 7th day
Thoughts of who would keep his creation his way
So god did ask his angel's first; to take care of the land
But they just shook their heads, put them in the sand
Hand's hidden under their wings…
Gabriel said, "It's too hard, not for us, we do so many other things."
So god he hatched a plan
…he created a superman
With no need for glamour nor armour
And he simply named him 'FARMER'.
To feed the people across his land
To till the soil with hoe in hand.
To endeavour to work when others stop
To make sure food is forever in the shop.
With hand's strong enough to carry a bail
And fix the roof with hammer and nail
But the same hands can gently pull a lamb
From a ewe
To work in pain, nor give in to cold and flu.
Finding energy harvesting long after dark
And up again milking cows well before the lark
Fixing machines on his back
Broke down on some old track.
Answering calls from a friend…
"Calf stuck in a birthing cow"
Needs some help, can you come now?
Farmers don't call it a favour
Just loves to help thy neighbour
Next week it may be him himself in need:

For farmers are a caring breed
Encouraging his children from an early age
Teaching farming life at every stage.
Then at the back end of the day
Even between loads of meadow hay;
Time together to eat their tea
For it's all about his family.
Then bedtime story he loves to do
And tucks them up with an "I love you".
Then back to work…hay to stack
Working fast before that thunders back.
Then after all is done…
lights out and off to bed
As his pillow hits his head…a thought of dread…
'I forgot to put the pig in it shed'
Up he gets puts them boots back on
For he will never leave job undone.
So if you do think you could do his job
Don't do it for pounds, pence or bob…
… It is done for the most caring boss
Who makes his sign by the way of a cross.

Hero

Bearded and broken
Hair that hasn't seen a comb
Newspapers and cardboard boxes for his home
Fingers knurled and crooked
Hooked around his bowl
As he offers it toward me and looks into my soul
Nails crow black skin grime pitted
Half hidden by fingerless gloves someone once knitted
As I looked back to his face
A smile came with a little grace
And from his tooth missing mouth he muttered these few words:
"Can you spare a bit cash for an old soldier?"
Well he had me there and then as my blood turned colder
I reached down, took his hand in mine and helped him to his feet
Now the day was cold
As the rain was taking hold
I walked with him to a cafe down the street
He limped though still had a grin
Through his tatty coat I could see he was thin
He sat right down by the door
Peeled off his gloves
A pocket book fell to the floor
I picked it up and offered it back
But his skin stretched hand waved me off
"Take a look it's who I am."
As he gazed towards the frying pan
"Bacon, beans and an egg if I may please…?
… And a tea, give the bag a bloody good squeeze"

His eye again gazed into mine
I opened his book; they began to shine
For what I was reading I could not believe
I was sat with a real live hero
Who fought for his country after ground zero
At Helmand he had taken the lead, what a man
To save his men
From the Taliban
Fighting and battling
Whilst dragging them out
When hit by a bullet, not even a shout
Four times he did go in the face of his foe
When he got home VC from the queen
At the palace with his wife on his arm and his girl on his knee
For being a hero and saving 3
I closed the book and I took one more look
As I asked him, "So why are you on the street?"
He bowed his head then looked to his feet
For I can't forgive myself for not saving four
The nightmares of battle and all the gore
Too much beer chased my family away
And on the streets I must stay
He finished his tea and walked to the door
Looked over his shoulder at me once more
With a tear in my eye
He said, "Do not cry."
I have conquered my fear
Turned his back and made off with his gear
Now every day I go home from the train
But as much as I've tried, that brave soldier, I have never seen
again.

True Love

When it comes, grab it and don't miss
You know you got it with that warm tender kiss
You don't walk just skip Cupid's arrow did not miss
That dragon deep down in your pit
Stirring don't want to feed yourself never mind it
Your finger tapping as time is dragging
Deep inside that dragons nagging
No time or need of sleep your heart is pounding and you're
not flagging
Time apart is the worst of all
Longing for your lover's call
Time stands still when not together
But is gone to fast in sun or worst of weather
You know you're in love when you can't sleep
Your lovers better than any dream no matter how deep
There is never a time or place for true love
It happens accidentally, in a heartbeat, and is sent from god
above
She is your guiding hand as you become her glove
You promise me you'll never forget me as you ask me never
to leave
For only when I die and then please do not grieve.
This is being truly in love
And if ever it happens to you stick with them
As they will stick with you.

Moon Light

Coal black burning thoughts
Of two loving burnt hearts
She takes my cold trembling hand
Softly tugging gentle as she asks, "Walk with me along the
sand."
Not a womanly sharp demand
So I walked on
Glancing at her in the moonbeams
As they Dance to and fro on cool crystal streams
Cutting through brandy butter sand
Shimming sea lures us as we turn away from land
I looked into her eyes all a glow
Water reflected moonlit lanterns leading where to go
I follow on as lamb would a sheep
For this is the woman I so what to keep
Leading me form land locked loneliness
Seaward to sail set bound for togetherness
"Moonlight take us as your prisoners and throw away the key
Only release us when she will marry me."

Broken and Bruised

Your older your beauty still there
Your tender sole is colder, stripped bare
Girlish thoughts that you once held so dear
The rudder that steered you through now damaged, your
future unclear
All because you gave your young naive heart for some
immature man to tear
Your ideas of womanly ways tore into a shred
Here you now sit alone broken bruised but not dead
Kitchen mopped school lunches done
Thoughts of…is this to be my only fun
Yearning for a deep husky voice to call you Hun
Well my lovely lady rise up from that chair
Cast of your chains climb out of yourself pitted nightmare
Remember back to your dreams
Before the arguments, shouts and screams
Fight, fight do not go gentle in to that ageing night
For you have dreams…have you forgotten
You were not put on god's great earth to remain downtrodden
So rise up daughter and live, how you wanted to
Find that real man that will love you.

Words Hurt

We all have regrets that we dwell upon
Maybe not taking that chance or caring for that certain someone
That lovely girl with that smile you should have kissed
Just as your phone rang, opportunity oh so missed
Your boy's first goal and football match
You couldn't say no to that second shift, more money you had to snatch
That night she stood at your door
Telling you she could take no more
You sat there remote in hand smiling thinking she won't go
Told her to hand you the key as she was leaving
She showed you, as now you sit there telly on not watching just grieving
Or that row with your dad
About the car, how you made him mad
Then left the house smiling no sign of remorse
Thinking as you drink your pint not your fault of course
Only to be called next morning, "Dad's died in his sleep."
You will carry that forever and how many times will you in your lifetime weep
The next I know happens far too often
It's not always, but mostly due to the woman's scoffing
Harsh words to her loving man
Maybe sometimes just cos she can
That night she says she has another lover
The night she should have chosen her words more careful
Instead she told him so unkindly and vengeful
Well lady as you must see
You sent that poor lad to the hanging tree

So let's think and count to ten
Not just women but bloody men
Words to some hurt as much as a smack
So before you leave and close the door and turn your back
Sort it out them words you've said
Always do it before you go upstairs to your bed

Grow Up

If you are a mum or dad
That won't promote your child seeing your ex how sad
Don't you think in some way your choice is bad
When you tuck your kids in tonight
Just as you kiss them before you switch off that light
Thinking as you must do
Are you doing it for them or you?
Remember before the little ones came along
You and them sang and danced to the same song
Come on let's stop the lie
Cos right now I'll tell you why
You would have pondered long and hard into the long
sleepless night
Was he or she the one…?
Mr. or Mrs. Right
Before you decided to add another into your life
Maybe as so many, you weren't man and wife
They say kids learn in the nest
Somewhere in your head you feel you're doing your level best
Perhaps the other doesn't do it right
Let's the kids down never in sight
That's for the kids to make the call
Not you…cos they missed taken the kids again to football
Some dads and mums are not the best, some are great too
Ask yourself why you're stopping them seeing the kids? Is it
because they wronged you?
This world is full enough of hate
Think back to yours and their first date
Did your heart beat so fast?
…as for them you couldn't wait

Think who you both once were and how things used to be
This is what your kids should only ever see
Grow up and sort it out
Then your kids may in times have a reflective shout.

The Princess of Darkness

She lives on St. Peter's Lane
Where watching, he bows his head in shame
As she causes families unbearable pain
She hatches her plans in her rented lair
Thriving off the hearts she loves to tear
Children are her unassuming bait
As she sits psychotically patient in her wait
Her prey are caring Grans and Grandads
After spawning children then turning on their dads
Their pain is her ultimate gain
Marinating their minds time is the key
Feeding off their dignity
Turning children against their kin
This is her despicable, wicked sin
Problem is she will never win
Cos I've been told by them from down below
That the Devil himself is too scared to let her in
St. Peter standing strong on his gate
Saying no way is she coming here and to tell her he can't wait
So she just watches though her window
Death and pain follow close beneath her shadow.
So young men listen hard to them that care
Find a woman sound of mind and in your children you will
share
Lucifer is the devil's kin
And in families pain she hope to win.

Why Can't I Say
What You All Think?

Why don't you "publicly like" that something that catches your eye
Well let me tell you why!
Cos we don't have a clue what's ok anymore
For fuck sake sorry I swore
You may be called racist sexist whatever the latest "ist" is
No place in this world for free thinking
Not any more straight speaking
Well who's to blame?
We are…what a crying shame
Scared and worried your thoughts you can't set free
Cos some meek fellow will disagree
Who was bought up soft and tame?
When things didn't go their way…Mummy says "complain"
Soft and spoilt the quitter's way
Taught in that nest not to try at every test
Too long on the parental tit
That's why they can't put up with the world and all it shit
Struggling in it and will never fit
Never encouraged or taught to find some grit
So that game that you think they should not play in
Just let them play and teach them they should try and win
If they don't teach them to grin
Bear with it…Don't give in
Tell them try harder
For god sake be a mother or father
Tell them they can do better
Cos if you don't you'll always have a quitter.

If I Should Die

When I go you all must know
I had my time to shine
I took my opportunities as they came along
With disappointments did try to stand up strong
Ladies came and left
Some stole my heart
Others I could not wait to depart
Some stay in my memories I think about each day
Others come in dreams and I ask them to stay.
Friends that stood by me all along the way
I thank you for it was not easy to fight for me each day
The talkers and mongers who do not have a life
They live in others and fed off my strife.
To them that want to cry standing in the Chapel
Ask yourself why?
…for someone who did each day his way
Never worried what he said to any problem fellow
Always in the sunlight never hiding in the shadow
Never looking back, Never bent or hollow
Up right and strong, straight as an arrow.
To friends that couldn't keep my pace, do not feel any guilt
…stick that smile back on your face
There were times I'd leave myself and go without a trace.
Maybe I have wronged some folks…just hope not too many
Regrets right now I have not any
Now I'm not planning to leave just yet
Hope I've got more time
To sing and dance with all of you
…as you make my life just fine.

Lost Son

If you see him in the park
Playing football after dark
Whistle to him for a lark
Tell him how we used to be
Before his mind was stole from me
Or even shopping at the store
Please before he leaves…stop him at the door
Tell him of me…how he was my shadow
Before she ploughed his little mind fallow
Then sowed her treacherous seed
For him to feed.
For she is foul and so unkind
Not sure she's of the human kind.
To all those who know me well
Help me now with the rat you smell
He needs me in his life as well
So go and ring the bell!
For we must stand, not stop and wilt
At them that lie and purge for our guilt
So honesty now turn the key
Now we may be free…
…to hold our heads with dignity.
For each to help in one and others tasks
Show them that hide behind their masks
It's time for us to stick together:
To give him and I am happy ever after.

Parc Y Mal

Parc Y Mal is where I go…
For when I need god to show
Here he fills me with his heavenly glow
For when I'm about to turn and face my foe
Not turn away when it best to go.
I think of what the gang would say
Always showing me the better way
In my times of trouble
And my friends there have been a few
I head to the farm by the dam
Tell them of my latest jam
Never judged or turned away
Always welcomed night or day.
Given council by all in parlour, barn and Norman's kitchen
…always listening never digg'in
Joy, Rachel, Nigel, Martin too…
But most of all Moira, I love you
You're wise and calm and very fair
And when I'm wrong you do not glare
Just a tut and then a prayer.
Sometimes I go when I'm not in trouble
And tea and cakes she always makes
She was first to see my farm not long after norm had left her
arm
As we drove I knew I'd done right
For in her words I'd seen the light
She likened me to norm
"a son of the soil"
Wow now that is an act I could not follow
So this poem is for you
The family that have always pulled me through.

Nights Are My Prison

Crow black stippled with stars
Who cares which one is Mars
The arm I rest my thought filled head upon…
Has no pulse for she has gone.
For this is horse hair filled, leather bound…
And eighteen inches from the ground
Stretched out here all alone
Like a dog that lost its bone.
But at least its home
Children in bed
Here I am no more tears left to shed
For she is gone…never to return.
My heart that was filled with all her fun…
Is only beating for I am numb
My love for her could not compare
…for why did I give her my heart to tear.
We first met in her yard
Which her parents they did guard
I picked her…thought she was prettier than her sister.
We were never apart
…In the tractor, truck and quad she would always sit upright.
Never a crossed word or fight
Chasing sheep in driving rain
Kicked by cattle…she felt no pain.
Moving the mob in summer's heat
Making my life so complete
Looking at me her gaze did never leave
Until now, oh I do grieve.
Loyalty she had in spades
Protecting lamb from foxes' raids

I miss my girl and her glare
Why did I give my heart for this dog to tear.
Tess is fine just in case you are worried.

Spring

It time to turn the page
As winter has left, with all its rage
Lambs are bleating in greening meadows
Caressed with the sun's loving glow
Honey bees start to buzz
Hunting for the flowers that bud
Sun is starting to stare
Eyes half open not a glare
Hedgehog and dormouse, squirrel too;
Are waking to the sounds of mallard rook and cuckoo.
Adder sits upon his stone
For its warm enough to leave his home
Foxes in their den
Cubs listening for sounds of men.
Mayfly larvae sits and waits doing other things
Too early for him to spread his wings.
Time to till and sow the seeds
Spread the muck and cut the weeds
Smells and scents carried on the warming winds
And listen to all the birds that sing.
Bats now leave their winter roosts
Moths to eat: a long awaited energy boost.
Puffins back from long off shores
…flying north overseas, no time to stop and pause
The owl now has young to feed time to hunt with sharpened claws
Flowers now start to bloom
And it will be summer very soon.

Poor Innocents of Yemen

Can't sleep in this bed
School trip running round in my head
All my Friends same to
Not sure where we're going, do you?
Up early not a fuss
Can't wait to get my seat on the bus
On we get chattering, full of noise
Lots of girls and lots of boys
Teacher tells us to find our seats
"Calm down or no treat"
And off we go in the blistering desert heat
But alas it Allah we must meet
Singing in an excited children's way
Not thinking in our lives we'll pay
Stopped for water and a drink
Bombed and murdered by who do you think?
It was sent from a Saudi plane
Bought from Britain France or Spain
Monies made
Will you makers feel the pain? No it's all about financial gain
Well take a look at what you've done;
You have butchered almost every one!
Do you feel any guilt?
Behind that desk on that chair you tilt
Not a hope you dealer of death
As the children take the final breath.
On your screens see class mates, shovels in hands…
…digging graves in the desert sand.
How can you as a man ever think it is right…?
…to bomb and kill with dynamite?

In far off land out of sight:
To profit from bombs, bullets, it's not your fight!
Well now it's time to stand and stare
For, in this war crime you must share
For it is real…no nightmare
Nobel got it right after he read he had died
Turned to the other side
Helping others to be kind
So how will you stop this slaughter?
Next it may be your son or daughter
And you will be handed a shovel
To dig their grave in clay or gravel.
Think before you sell your Napalm…
…with its death fowl glow
…that kills kids and not just your foe.
And you will have to answer to god and their mothers;
You're as bad as the trigger pullers.

Who Am I?

It's a calling from above
It's not for the faint of heart it is done for love
At its best you can hope you will stay sane
At its worst all you feel is so much pain.
The statistician say
It's the most dangerous job for killing you
Accident or suicide
Now I've given you a bit of a clue
(Got it yet?).
I am a professional…
For not many my work can do;
I do my work for all of you.
A doctor you may need twice each year
A lawyer maybe once but who's to say
But you will need me at least three times a day.
(Got it yet?)
I battle and cannot be seen to fail
In summer's heat and winter's Gail.
Viewed by outside folk…most think we're a big joke
Though some do think you're a decent bloke.
Everyone thinks we are rich…granted some are
But most are not by far.
(Have you got it yet?)
In rain and sleet you have to work
When snow and ice are sent to freeze…
…those two imposters love to tease.
Through pain and flu;
Even when death visits, taking loved ones from you.
No time to stop you have to work on through
Grieving is done

In your head
If you're lucky when you get some time in your bed.
Darkness is not a time for you to rest
Sometimes it's when you must be at your best.
(Got it yet?)
We meet death along the way
We see miracles every day.
Our clock it is here
For we mark time not by minute or hour, but seasons of the year.
(Must have it by now but if not?)
In fields of green we ply our trade
Raising cattle on grass our forefathers laid.
On hillside, glen, even reclaimed fen
Land made of flint clay and dark red soil
To grow your food, with all our toil.
To produce good food from our gate…
…so you can feed it to your family on a plate
(Yes a farmer)

Puku: A Tongan Narberth Man

What a day Puku
Hope we did you proud
By the way thank you to that Narberth crowd
You guys reminded me how important you are to me and so
very loud
You got us to the final
Bell
But god my broken body hurts like hell
What a game though
All over 40
Played very hard but never dirty
Played the Tongan way, god watching from upon high
Sure I heard his mighty sigh
As Puku scored the final try
Puku I hope you had a great birthday
You taught us Narberth boys to play the Tongan way
Only right now I got a date with a bath
Cos being tackled by you Tongan men is not bloody laugh.

Muddling and Moaning

All day I tend to my land and stock
So why would you be such a cock
Sitting or nosing muddling and moaning
Where do you get the time?
I don't commit any crime
Only to work from dawn till dusk
And tend to my stock as I must
But you're like the buzzard that sores
Looking for wrongs it's your crazy cause
The field you wonder
Off the path stealing my berries they are not yours
If I was found in your veg patch
Taking a cauli would that be a match
No it would be a call to the police
And I'd be fined for a breach of the peace
And your dogs that chase my stock if I shot them dead, dropped at your door
That may even the score
But I let them go with a foot up the arse
Never a sorry, not your fault of course
And when you fly tip your cutting and grass
You're now getting to be a pain in the ass
So I tip my hat and try again cos here in the country we aren't as insane
So I wave to you at your gate
No reply
Cos you're off like a shot to your phone
That why
To ring the council to be a pain
Cos you can't drive your car with shit on the lane

Really lady why did you come from the town to the country
you so fucking dumb
So as my patience starts to wane
I look for my gun to ease your pain
That's how we deal with moaners and a horse that's lame
Out of their misery
"Oh what a shame"
But even with my mind in a spin
I think to the past and then generations before
Who've seen your type here before?
Sooner or later they will close your door
In a pine box you'll go
And we'll see you no more
And we will still be here on our land
Happy and smiling, feeling just grand
Cos you moaners and groaners are missing the point
You spend all of your life trying to bait
Missing the beauty of this land you could paint
But you moan and groan then it's too late
Your words and claims will be gone like you
And we're still here with work to do
Feeding other in towns (thank god) just like you.

Withybush Hospital

Why would you close the counties only hospital?
Where so many strive each day to save others in such a
selfless way
They don't just work for their monthly pay
For the stress and pain they endure
Cuts from bosses at the top…that will never cure.
They don't have a clue
Well let me tell you who fooling who
Cos the nurse on the ward is trying so hard
She's never fills in an overtime card
The porter and cleaner that too toil so hard
…worried when they'll be getting an unemployment card.
Divided and conquered, morale is on the floor
Then managers have the cheek to ask them for more.
Under staffed you men at the top like that way
Cos a nurse will do the work of two and only one you have to
pay.
Time to get your arses out of your chairs that tilt
No you just sit wallowing no sign guilt.
You should do what is right and roll up your sleeves…
Stick on those scrubs and start to please.
From the front you must lead
Instead you're the leach that this hospital you do bleed.
If you talk of closing it down
No doctors will make a home in our town
So its locum's you pay
Which cost more for him for one day
Than a full time doctor who'd love stay.
You blame the assembly government…they blame White
Hall

All the while Crabb sideways under his rock he does crawl.
Well tell him the next time he wants your vote:
He has been as useful as a boat that don't float
Sold down the river, by snakes that slither.
We are being forgotten…down trodden
By the stand backers, the back stabbers, the bull Shitters
It's rotten.

No More, Stop This War

Children want a playful life
So why give him so much strife
Yes you once were my wife
But that was in a different life
We once loved and laughed
We were happy
God gave us OUR little chappy
He has bought us so much joy
OUR fantastic little boy
Then things turned sour as sometime they do
I'm not here blaming you
Just asking with all my heart
Why oh why is your only goal to keep my son and me a part
The energy you have spent on your crusade
Day after day manipulating trying to persuade
For god's sake he is OUR son
Not yours or mine he needs everyone
Grans and Grandads
Brothers and sisters Aunts Uncles Cousins Too
Not only folks and family decided by you
So come sit with me and talk
Or take OUR son for walk
Not to squawk and shout
But to both listen and sort it out
This should not be a battle
Remember he is OUR son not a chattel
What are you ever hoping to gain?
By putting him me my family though so much pain
There are no winners, it's not a game
Played out each day frame by frame

I know you have it in you to stop this fight
For now it's time to do things right
Not harassment orders or hiding in the courtroom shadow
But show some old fashioned grit
And cut out all this shit
Here I am white flag in hand
You can take it as you will "Victory" but it's not a demand
For now it's down to you and as all to see
Because right now you have me on bended knee.

Son

I'm not around right now
Not there, for you, to show you how
So I've set down onto paper some important rules to get you
through your life:
Son, you must always keep you cool
Not something I've always done but it's me that been the fool.
I need you to think and keep your head...
...no matter what being said.
Son, fists are not always right
So please if you can...always avoid a fight
Always trust yourself even if it's only you
When others sing a different tune
But don't knock them for it or lose any sleep
For I didn't bring you up to follow like a sheep.
Folks will always tell you lies;
Twisting your words for their own ends to your surprise.
Just don't give way to fools who never play by the rules.
Just stay strong; the truth will always come out...
...no need to stand and shout.
It's good to look your best and smart
But please don't ever be a tart.
Don't try to bullshit as you may have done with me
And how I told you, you can't bullshit a bullshitter, cos that
bullshitter was me!
Some will hate along the way
But hating is for them to do and say
You don't have hate in you
Let only the good shine through.
Dreams they will lead you as you grow
...you must follow but know when it's time to let them go.

In life's path you will win and lose
Neither one you can choose
And when they happen treat them both the same
…that way you will feel less pain.
As you know before you went away
I told you of our family and how we had to pay.
As we had hard times along the way
We lost everything and were quite poor
But it didn't break us that's for bloody sure!
Money don't make you happy
You will find that out soon enough my little chappie
And if you ever think its good times all the way
You're in for one hell of a shock one day.
Sure as shit sticks to my shovel
And in the dirt or trouble
You are going to have to grovel.
Well that's the only time to hate, you will know why
It's there deep down that fire in your belly and hatred in your eye…
…all put there by me on the sly.
And if you still think you're going to fail:
Remember you're a
(Any sir name)
Now fight on tooth and nail.
When the bad times are behind you
Never worry about them again
You know how to beat them; it's just a bloody game.
I am always here for you, son…at any time of day
Please pick up that phone and speak to grand pa hay.
Always remember son you gave me so much joy
When you become that man you will still be my little boy.
Please believe me your mother caused all this pain.
And I will always love you until we meet again.

What Is Being British?

It is pride in your flag…
Not setting it alight for you to then drag!
It is singing in your church or chapel
Not listening to your priest telling you, your sabre you must rattle.
It is not the colour of your skin; black, brown or white
It's about not showing up with dynamite.
It is obeying our laws
Not treasonous words spoken behind closed doors.
It is being able to have free speech
Not the radical poison you preach.
It is to be tolerant to all
Not just your own wanting for others to fall.
It is to work and build, earning your slice of the cake
Not shirking, stealing, being a snake.
It is about helping others and community…
… Not planning for your anarchy.
It is about stepping up and doing good…
… Not hiding in your neighbourhood.
It is to love your son and daughter…
… Not marry them off like lambs to slaughter.
It is to love woman kind…
… Not cover her up out of sight and out of mind.
It is pulling together in the same direction…
… Not scheming insurrection.
It is about humanity…
… Not your bloody mutiny!
In Britain we put our toe on the line and face our enemies…
… Not suicide bombers for sovereigns to please.

You will understand if you're British: others have tried to bring us to our knees
And it's not for our god but our country that we duly appease.
We want you to be part of this great country no matter your creed or colour
As long as you can pull with us together.
The important stuff is the same in both our books…
… But it's purged and changed by imposters and crooks.
So let's sit together and figure it out
Before bloodshed and war of that there will be
I have no doubt.
So come let's do it whilst we're still in with a shout
And let's be British and SORT IT OUT!

Head or Heart

Which one is for fools
Use either and you break the others rules
If the heart is pulling you
And the head doesn't have a clue
The heart will always pull you through
But if the heart is pulling you to your surprise
While the head is very wise
The heart will always fail
The head will prevail
Only when the heart feels real love
Even if the head is in charge
For the head will follow like the horse tows the barge
And if the heart is led by someone who's aim is not to please
Just to hold you in a hate full squeeze
The head will quicken its pace
To catch you in a saving embrace
Persuading you to stop others from hurting you
Then there is the dangerous heart
That the mightiest head can't overrule
And in the worst of company it will test
For in its perfect storm it will ruin the best
Then there is the saddest of all
The lonely loveless fool
Who's head strong thoughts will always rule
They will forever pay
For they will always chase love away
Now we need both head and heart in equal measure
But I feel that love is the biggest treasure
So follow your heart every day

The head will learn to follow and not stray
But most of all your lover may just stay.

Young Men Do the Bidding

Why do men in power do such things
Sending boys to do their bidding
Hiding behind their desks f...king grinning
For it was not like this in the beginning
Men In power won respect leading and winning
They would never give a man a job to do
That they themselves could not see through
From the front they would ride with trusted men by their side
Then after they would sit
Talk making sense of it
Would not send young men out to die in trench or under Afghan sky
That's because boys don't ask why
They just go do their duty as they try
So now it's time to turn the tide
Through the doors open wide
Tell them cowards behind the desk, "Now who's grinning?
For you are coming to do your own bidding."
For we have come here today for you
Let's just see how you do
Leading men in time of war
To fight and battle in this gore
Let's see if you stand your ground as men are lay dying all around
No jaw jaw for this is war
No pen or quill to sign away your day
It's in blood and guts that you will pay
And let's see if you live through that battle
Then Back in Whitehall with your toffs will you again sabre rattle

And come again to the front
Stand with men at your back and charge on head long
screaming "ATTACK"
If we do and win the day
Forever men will stand and stay
With their lives prepaid pay.

Why Does It Happen?

Nobody is immune
And I can't see it stopping any time soon
Everyone has experienced its bite
Some even returned it
To others…
You have! You know I'm right
We are all capable of hurting others
So now sisters and brothers
Where is the line and what's your gain
For bulling is enjoying others pain
It's done to all by all
Not just with a punch but out of sight or with a call
From behind a screen from miles away
Not just on the bus to work each day
In the yard of the village school
Or a banker's board room by some high powered fool
Now I can only speak for me
I was bullied by two or three
But they did not get the better of me
I could name them on this paper with my pen
At the time they were children now they are men
I have watch them grow
In their lives they did not show
Two were jailed for heinous crimes
The third I lost track of but heard he's found better times
They did not as many do, drive me to a rope and knot
Just placed a seed that I've tried but never forgot
The bits of me I did not want to see
The tough outer shell
The one that most of you know well

The one I found easiest to sell
But as I age and do not need that cloak
I find there is beneath, a very different bloke
Not that I would change too much of the other
Let just say he has found his more loving brother
After 40 years of keeping in hidden behind a wall bullied given
I find that in me again at last
I can look at my past
I not saying that it hasn't helped me shape my present
But god at the time it was so unpleasant
In fact I used that word was used just to rhyme
When really I had a fucking horrid time
And I'm not saying that things I've done to others, could be seen as mean
But a bully I hope I've never been
If you read this poem and you are in need
Because some bulling bastard has planted that seed
Please don't look to rope and tree
Or barrel of a gun please come see me
You have nothing to lose and all to gain
Because others love you why leave them in pain.

TB Test Tomorrow

Thoughts of dread filling his head
Darkness his only friend in that bed
Where sweats and worries stop his sleep
Till wife upstairs she did creep.
He'd heard her on the phone;
To their only daughter for a moan
As she lay by his side, holds him with a comforting arm
"It's alright love no badger on our farm."
No there weren't and that's for sure…
… But that didn't stop TB coming to his neighbour's door.
Eyes wide open just to stare
In to the darkness and a best beware:
For thoughts of bills, how many will go, starts to scare.
Eyes start to close
As the cock starts his waking crows
Sun's eyes opening, starts to stare
Before it's full on glare
Thursday morning, cattle calling
Calf's jumping all around
But where's the farmer?
He can't be found
He sits at kitchen table… TB test reading…is he able?
Knock knock on the door, like the condemned man
It's the hang man of that I'm sure
"The vets here love" comes the call
Up he gets, standing tall
Wellies on stick in hand
Start's his workman, with his wilful command
80 down and not a lump
40 left still in a grump

Lights his fag
Takes a fear filled drag
10 more down and still a frown
5 more done 5 to go
Is that a smile starting to show
4 still left
Vet takes a sharp intake of breath
"What is it man?"
"A lump" callipers out
Under his breath it's to god he doe's shout
A long pause
"It's ok open the doors"
3 and 2 through very fast
Then there's only one the last
Farmer and vet look at each other
"It's fine Fred clear test…"
"Great don't know what's all the bother"
Came from the kitchen for she is the farmer's wife
Who carries so much stress and strife…
The wind beneath his wings that easies his flight
But guys do we ever do it right?
The wife is there out of sight, putting up with all our shite.

Courage

It comes in many ways
Of course it's in a solider…head long he will charge
Shells falling all around him, from enemy's barrage
Or the life boat and it crew that launches without an ask
Into a venomous sea
Volunteers all, out to do their lonely task
Or the fire fighter running into a burning hell
While everyone is leaving at the sound of a bell
Our bobby on the beat
Unarmed as he wonders the dark and dangerous street
Courage it also comes in so many forms as you will agree
Like the poor child that is blind and does not see
That smiles every morning as mum cries in her tea
The dad with his two year old sitting on his knee
Who knows without a transplant his little girl will not see
three
The lad who cares for his two younger brothers and hides
them from the shame
As his mother sticks a heroin filled needle in to take away her
Pain
The child in the school yard kicked and beaten day after day
By some big bully's just because they think he's gay
Well courage is in us all
As babies we got back up after every bump and fall
In life we lose and get knocked down
Is it failure?…well some may say
Well I say you only fail if it's on the floor you stay
This is when our courage comes and picks us up each day
Other to their church they go preying to their god
stirring up their courage…

While none believes think them odd
Well whichever way it comes from deep within your sole
Just be very thankful as courage digs you out of the deepest
darkest hole.

Judge

Who sits and interprets our law
Because right now you're so poor
You are lost and such a bore
Did you really study law year on year
When you took your oath did you listen? Before you swore
Behind that bench hammer in hand
Get your wigged up Privileged head out of the sand
For you have had no life to have taken lessons from
Just Eaton then oxford
So how can you sit and judge? Come on
Do you know the likes of us?
Do you hell, you've never taken a bus, drank in our pub or
tasted our grub
Been bathed with your brother in some old tub
Ran with the kids through the roughest of streets
Then in to a bed without any sheets
For you know nothing of the law of the street
To hustle each day, lucky your kids may eat
How can you send a man down?
Sitting up there under our queen's crown
Right now I'd be happier judged by coco the clown
With him pedos and rapists would get the gun bullet in the
head, there job done
The men at the top politicians and bankers
Bunch of thieving wankers
Why when they steal do they not get clink
Really judge you best have a think
Worst still they keep their jobs
Do you posh Eaton boys really think we're all knobs?
To sit here in our street

Treated like shit under your feet
For if you don't change
We will turn over...to a new page
Then you will see rage
Upright and strong
It's time to march with the throng
Time for change
No more to be down trodden
By you rich so rotten
We refuse to be the forgotten.
And we will throw open your unjust court room door
And your biased hammer will fall no more.

Woman, Do You Really Know Man?

I'm that man that lays by your side
That worries about you, eyes open wide
Thinking of the things we need each day
How much they cost and how I will pay
Years ago it was not this way up at sun rise
Hunting and gathering meat was the prize
Boy how things have moved on there's no stopping
Household bills kids' clothes and shoes not forgetting weekly
shopping
But in us men will you "love" please agree
Really I was made for hunting see
That's why we fall out sometime I shout
Cos working in this job
Frustrations take hold of me from deep in my hunter's sole
I feel I'm trapped in this deep dark hole
Yours has always been the material way to bare the
children…the mother's way
My life's work long ago
Was to hunt and fight to keep you safe from our foe
Now redundant from that task
So I work hard have to wear a different mask
Domesticated dogs still bite
And some days I boil over I know it isn't right
For you put up with all my site
So when again I come home to our cave
You start on that you're my bloody slave
Cooking, cleaning while I sitting my feckin chair
Just before you turn bad, just as your beautiful eyes start to
glare

Put down that poker and come sit with me on my chair
Cos darling I love you and in this crazy world, my life with
you
I want to share.

Apart

As he sat by the kitchen range
His head filled with how much will change
No more would she shuffle
While bringing in coal with the scuttle
Her smell was still in the air
Her knitting was there on her chair
As he sat head in hands
Trying so hard not to cry
As others made whispered plans
He knew what they were planning to put him through
But right now what could he do
All he could think about was his Tilly, his princess
And fifty six year of happiness
He could hear her plain as day
How was that?
Cos yesterday we buried her deep in Christian clay
Again he heard her voice whispering
"Love you have a choice, don't let our kids tell you what is
right
Send them home we will talk tonight."
Stan scratched his head and wobbled to his feet
"Now kids I love you very much but tonight
I want you gone for I am meeting with someone."
Well his children did not agree
And protested to stay with him
So Stan stood shoulders back shouted loud
"It's my house and I want it back."
So they did go one by one
And Stan was proud of what he done
Cos see Tilly was the strong one

Tuff as teak with everyone
But then he remembered teary eyed
That just last week she had died
So he moved the knitting off her chair
Sat in it and started to stare
It wasn't long before he heard her claim
"See that bastard cats back in again."
Smile came to Stan face
For he loved it when she put him in his place
Then her words turned to him
"I'm sorry love that I'm am gone
And I do miss you and everyone
But see love I was in pain
And I know you and I will soon meet again."
Stans hand reached out to touch her hand
But she was gone
He could not tell anyone
They would think him mad
For kids already talking now of how he's to cope
Sitting round just to mope
Well Stan he hatched a plan
He asked god to take him too
So he sat in her chair
Closed his eyes with a little prayer
And it wasn't long before he sensed her there
Next he reached out and this time felt her touch
Thank you thank you Lord so very much
As St Peter opened the gate
Stan walked to Tilly he could not wait
Tilly just sat with a glare and said
"Stan you bloody lout
Before you left you didn't put that bastard cat out."

County Lines

So the gangs are coming to our patch
Do they think we will be their match?
Or sit on our arses and scratch
In our town you folks must know
Crack cocaine is starting to make its horror show
Dads are you going to stand by?
Or take a walk find a dealer and ask him why
Lead him to the station with a firm hand
Before your son or daughter end up in the Promised Land
Or are you going to sit there in your chair
And wait to see your loved ones addicted and become your
worst nightmare
If you think them boys in blue can do the job
Now let me tell you you're a bloody knob
Being a Community is how you win
Best start soon cos we have already let them in
Them that read this poem and like their coke
Don't laugh cos let me tell you it ain't no joke
Your habit is what they seek
And they prey on children and the meek
All because you folks are so weak
Them dealers love you that way
So you can snort, getting stoned and high night and day
And it's not just in your money you will pay
As you stand and cry
Watching your loved ones next to die
It is not just in the city
Now they're here and their kind don't fucking pity
They will just turn our beautiful town dark and shitty
So I'm asking the men among you stand

Let's become a ruthlessly band
Cos brothers your kids will be next
If you don't sort out the vermin and pest
I write this poem for my friend you all know him well
He is fighting to keep his family together cos of drugs that they sell
It is hurting them and they are going through unspeakable hell
He is hard and strong and would never give in till the bell
He would not ask for help or favour
But we all have to come together and STAMP OUT there antisocial behaviour
Keep your eyes open and ears too
But most of all come together as a community we must do.

Where Is the Sense

Is it the way things are to become
No more clapping when having fun
Can you be proud to be white?
Can you hell, it just not right
Check with your lawyer before that girl your about to kiss you
romantic fool
You just may be breaking some sexual rule
In a country that's gone PC mad
It's not even cool to be a lad
It's the same for girls too
Not sure now which loo is for who
And now girl guides are for boys too
And I see your all posting you're not a racist tool
But really do you have to…
Wouldn't you think that's a given rule
Just this week a 72 year old granny taken to court for putting
balloons up for her grandson she doesn't see
Cos his psychotic controlling mum says, "Grans harassing
me."
Really CPS.
You are why this great country is in a fucking mess
History and stories having to be rewritten
Please you can't change the past that a given
We all know slavery was not right
But you can't change what has happen and their plight
And all the folks that did things wrong…it was back then
We can't change the facts good or bad with the stroke of a
liberal pen
We all know that it takes all sorts to be a great country gay
straight lefty's rights black, brown, white, yellow

Sorry if I've missed you out but doesn't mean I'm a bad fellow
We are trying too hard to do it right
God is watching out of sight
Scratching his head and asking…why?
Saying do away with them lawyers as he sits upon high
They make life so complicated only for them to gain
While souring above waiting to swoop on our pain
They try to convince us of their ridiculous made up PC laws
So they can snatch your money with their vulturous claws
So let's try an old approach
Granny had this saying inscribed in to her broach
"You can't please everyone all of the time
So bloody get on with it and let's all start to shine."

Wishes

I wish that them that do
Don't
I wish them that can
Would
I wish them that didn't
Did
I wish them that wanted
Had
I wish them that think
Thought
I wish them that listen
Talk
I wish them that say
Do
I wish they that teach
Learn
I wish them that sleep
Dream
I wish them that need
Have
I wish them that are led
Lead
I wish them that have
Give
I wish them that see
Tell
I wish them that hear
Say
I wish them that laugh
Cry

I wish them that hate
Love
I wish he finds
She or she finds he
I wish most of all

Young Boys

Just left school broke ever rule
Still scratches on my knees from rugby in the park
But now I'm on the train on my own and it's after dark
On my way from Eaton
Next stop Biggin Hill
Daddies got me a spot flying spitfire oh what a thrill
"Off that train."
There he stood 6 ft 6
Barrel chested, eye patch and cane
"On that lorry you privileged gentlemen this is the RAF not a
bloody jolly."
Bellowing like a rutting bull
For now we'd met flight Sergeant major Gull
Looking down at me, he growled, "In the front, the back is
full."
I open the door and climbed in
As did he under his moustache I saw him grin
As he took the wheel
by the station light I glanced his hands huge and knuckles like
lumps of steel
I stayed dumb for at school that was the rule of thumb
As we drove my eyes began to shut I nodded off
Woken by a shooting pain; for gull had hit me with his cane
"Sleeping and you want to fly a plane
When you're up in the sky for hour upon hour no sleeping up
there, best you work on your will power."
We drove for miles in near total darkness
I was starving and hoped for food at the officers' mess
"Out you gets my little privileged pets your all mine now."
He was right for from that night

It was his duty to keep us right
He taught us how to loop the loop
And in a dog fight how to shoot
As after six long weeks he had taught us all he could
He saw us off some never to return gone for good
So for all those young boys and that's was what we were
Battling in the summer's skies how we loved to soar
For we were so few, they had more
But we were good and evened the score
Our boys had done us proud
turned those Nazis homeward bound or sent them spiralling
to the ground
So on the next summer's day gaze up into a cloud
Think about those brave lads it's got to make you proud.

To Be Welsh Is God-Given

Men for whom we should be proud
That left their mark all around.
Merlin had king Arthur's back
With magic he had a knack.

Owain Glyndwr
was never beaten
All the English could do was call him…
The Heathen.

Henry Tudor Pembroke boy
To Bosworth Field he did track
Where Richard the third he did sack.

Seven welsh men have been president of the USA
But not down to them it's turned out this way
Charles rolls of Rolls Royce fame
Was welsh and he loved to claim.
At Rorkes Drift well out numbered
The welsh boys stood their ground
Zulu worriers, shouting with spears all around…
Men of Harlech booming out
Scared the Zulus and we did rout.

Colliers, steel workers and farmers too
Hard men that shaped our land
Turned our dragon into a colossal brand
Our coal is world's best.
Our steel stands very test.

NHS founder Nye (Aneurin) Bevan a Welsh national treasure;
He gave Health care to all in equal measure.
Our greatest love is of the oval ball
And the best player ever of them all
A welsh man through and through.
Gareth Edwards…with the ball he knew just what to do.
Choirs and singers we have the best
Full of Welsh passion, hwyl and zest;
We love our beer and song and would never think to ratio.
Rugby is our religion and our stadium is the proof
…by the way it's got a roof.
From our rugged coast to our highest mountain
When Wales win you will hear the shouting
So we are Welsh happy friendly and more
…careful mind this dragon can raw
So as you tuck your children in to bed
Put this thought in their head
Be welsh, be proud, and most of all when you sing
do it loud

I Am Not Gone, I Was There

Sitting there in the family room
Pale green walls don't hide the gloom
Tissue holding in a sweating palm
Plastic coffee cup doesn't calm
I was there knelt at your side running my finger though your tear stained hair
I stroked your hand as you waited for the doctor in the gallows chair
As you listened while your beating heart was starting to tear
Doctor telling you I was gone
Well he was wrong I was there in sprit that shone
The next three days I did not leave your side
Watched you cry and from our friends wanted to hide
Stood with you no words I could utter
Watched a tear fall from your cheek on to your toast you tried to butter
Listening to your sobbing words "it's not fair!"
How I want you to know I was there
At the service in our Chapel
No tambourine did you rattle
Our boys stood and spoke of me
I was there if only you could but see
In the pulpit John and James my hands on their shoulders not just two but us three
Now six months have passed and you're doing well
But there's something I do so want to tell
Johns about to be a dad
That's not all the next may make you sad
It's time for me to leave you it's not for good
So live your life…I'd love to have stayed if I only could

I will see you very soon in a short while, a blink of an eye
I'm not gone this is not good bye.

What Is Loss?

Is it pain that no pill can stop the ache
When all your friends say give yourself a shake
Is it when each night you lay awake
When all your dreams and ambitions are just fake
Wishing to be rid of this unimaginable pain
Sapping the life out of my broken soul just existing as I drain
Where is the happiness and my smile
They left me said "we will back in a while"
A child's while has long since gone
It has been so long since I have shone
While upon while have come and gone
Since I laughed and sang with everyone
She left without a trace
Why was she taken
Into God's grace
No more the touch of her hand
How can our children
ever start to understand
No more beach walks
No more pillow talks
No more watching gulls that sore
No more listening to the seas distant raw
Alone and broken I must fight
And bring our children up…
…"do it right"
As she always told with such glee
Come on god help and carry me
For I need your strength to help set her free
For loss is felt by everyone
The hopelessness when they are gone

It's the same for strong and meek
When at the time the futures so bleak
But from somewhere in us we find the strength to march on
And as we do over time that pain is gone
Just loving memoirs of how you shone.

Wild Son

A wild colt makes a good horse…well that's what the old
folks say
Some say it calmer when you have a son with will and is a
charmer
But I would much rather, in this world full of sheep…
A lad with spirit and character
With gravel in his gut
And spit in his eye
Not one who would lay down and cry
But how do you coax?
That child when he is out of control and running wild
…not a candidate for the naughty step is this child
A clip well to my cost—I know that's wrong
For I was judged by the characterless throng
How many of us have had to discipline when what they said
may be true and had to hide the smile that's we do?
Never letting on when he's bad
At those things he will say that makes such sense and make
you sad
But we have to bring him down to earth
Cos we are the father
That's what we do
But how many of us can say truly it's not something we enjoy
each day
"Too big for them boots", "You're getting too clever", I was
told
But somehow I was still allowed to be bold
The secret is how far to go before they lose the seed that you
did sow
Remember that "the acorn never falls far from that tree"

And we all love to hear from someone who says with glee:
"I see you in he."
That's why as much as you try you are meeting yourself in your son
…and as much as you want but can't admit it, it's so much fun
So love yourself as much as your son
…and if he stays that way your work is done.

God or a Bang

It's a question only we ask
more often than not as we take our final gasp
So I put this to us all when you're next having that dread filled
day
How many times will we say, Help me god
Never do we utter the words big bang I am so in need
So why is that?
Maybe parents or school sowed a seed
Or is it that we look each day
Did god's bang create everything this way
the air we breathe, all the food we need
Even Science tells us they don't have the answers or equations
To show us how they say it happened, just theories and
blarney
To confuse and make us weary
I'm not a god fearing man but as I age and look for answers
knowing there's no second chances
I start to be seduced by nature's advances
The bee in the hive would never survive without the rose
And the flowers that grow and thrives would never be alive
without the power of the hive
Not to mention chicken or the egg
So did it all start with an atom that did so conveniently part
Or a something we have called god
Who tried so very hard to make this earth we live on
It's us with the questions
But he won't answer for his good intentions
He gave us our thoughts and wisdom
But eventually these will destroy his kingdom

So now I have only one thought who of us is strong enough,
To stop and save at all this wonderful stuff
The bird that sings this grass that grows
the cool breeze that blows
Our children words so thoughtfully said as we tuck them into
bed
Who gave us all these precious things?
It was done with thought of that I'm sure
But whoever did it there was a flaw
He gave to us our mind to think and reason
So why have we used them for war and treason
Our earth we were not given but loaned by a loving guardian
Who trusted us to keep?
Is in this heavens oh how he must weep?
So is there time to stop this crime, to dry his tears
To look after our planet and calm his fears
For it was lent for us to look after let's not be the generation
That historians tell
How we let it all go to hell
We must use our god given talents and reason
Then he may pardon us for our treason.

The Vote

Men in power we put there
But we don't know the man…for how can we?
It's not like he turns up for a cup of tea…or a pint of beer or
even G&T
No we are all told that he is bold by his party
His speeches to which we all listen
Are not his words but party written
But how do we ever know the man…
Really how do we know he can?
If I wanted to be represented in things that really matter;
I'd call a mate who I know and trust
Not someone with the parties' lust
We all vote for a party that are all full of hot air and guff
They never follow through with stuff
Red, blue, green or white none of them get it right
I'm of the mind the men that they give us
Are there for the money fame or a power buzz
Because let's be honest and that we can…
…because we all have a plan
Now that right they call the vote
Right now it as useful as a piano that can't sound a note
It's not about power for the man in the street
The nurse in the ward tired and rushed off her feet
The student in college that is in so much dept just to gain a
little knowledge
Or our mums with their mop
No it's for the men at the top;
The Fast talkers the side steppers the back stabbers
The bull shitters the stand backers the expense fiddlers
I could go on for an age

But now is time for change
…the man in the street to vote with his feet
Let's not bother voting at all for any of them
Just once let's show 'em and then they may have to
Let us get to know 'em and we can make our minds up who they are:
ask them questions…ones they never answer
Let's just see who is a chancer
And if when you met 'em and you think they are genuine
Let us forget about parties it's all to tribal
Let's give them the tasks and make them liable
Don't pay them with money, we will give them a zero hour contract
Productivity based with SSI pay
Let us see how they like it that way
Only the best will give it a try
No Eaton boys would want to know…
"Wouldn't that be such an awful show."
And if they are not what they said
…and we were all misled
Then instant dismissal they will get
Just like us and all the rest
Not fingers crossed and hope for the best
Find that straight talker and a walk walker
And maybe we can say with pride:
That all the folks who died to gets us the vote did not die in vain cos our country can claim
That we have our say once again.

Time

Times they may change
But why do men as they age need more?
…not to say we all start that way with bills to pay
as we age and plough our furrow
…never thinking of tomorrow
Do we look back as our children grow…
Never looking over our shoulder
As they grew and got older
We say it's what we do
Well now who fooling who?
Parties missed football too
goals scored without you
In our hearts we know what true
They really DO need you
For what is learned in the nest…
Working worrying shouting too
not enough time for an "I love you":
will be their compass as they grow
to their offspring they will show
So why be a sheep? Off to work as they sleep
…home at dark you must creep
for do not wake them, they are fast asleep
I know all this too well
I hear you saying, "What the hell?"
But am freed from that spell
You can too
But it's not easy… That is true
Needs some thought so push on through
Monies needed I do agree
But time with loved ones has no fee

And let's be honest you will pay
when your children leave some day.

Swallows...

Butler coloured feathers how apt
For they work in service, they never stop
…it's their young that keeps them on the hop
It's a hell of a thing…
When you have to drink on the wing
Spit fires of our summer skies
To feed their young with tonnes of flies
Dancing and jiving as they sing
Oh they do give flight a romantic ring
But not for our pleasure do they soar
It's down to parenthood of that I am sure
On the wing over deserts 5000 miles
Fighting heat for most of the trip, such a feat
To reach our long lit summers days, but when they do arrive
There is no time for them to rest
Time to fix their broken nest
Of spit and mud, Stuck to the barn beam or piece of wood
What price would Rolls Royce pay to have his engine for one day
So next time they swoop and loop the loop at picnic, party or by the chicken coop
Think what start their chicks have had
…that's why they don't turn out so bad.

Farmers

Who would work from dawn till dusk
In winter gale and summer dust
In driving rain
Hand so calloused that feel no pain
No time for stress days off
Like most jobs paid by a forgiving boss to staff that don't give
a toss.
Now a farmer's life is lonely and grim
No sick pay for him
And them that say he gets a subsidy
Well take it away and we will see
just who bleats when the house wife can't pay
for her meats on Christmas Day
means she will have to forgo her treats
Hair doos and nails that phone and emails, spar breaks and
trips on the rails
Cos it not for a farmer the subsidies came, it was to feed the
nation cheap
So our great country can could get back on its feet
after war came and did its worst
So now get rid and pay the price no monies left for things nice
Cos it will cost you at least thrice
or keep your own cow and see just how long you could keep
it alive and try to survive like the farmer has too
As well as all that the farms that you see all green and weed
free
is done for no fee
By proud strong men from fen to the glen
And when they do worry, no one comes in a hurry
they are left to sort them out on their own

As how they been shown
Passed on from father to son
And more often than not them that were not turn to
the Barrel of a gun
So next time you eat and start to bleat
Think of the men who do not cheat
To bring you your meat
And the countryside that make you smile
Just say thanks once in a while.

Alone

Here she sat all alone
Darkness filled the room and her soul
She could hear her cat lapping water from its bowl
No more cash in the pot
It was only Wednesday and she had spent the lot
But only one more night in her island chair
Only twelve hours marooned sat up right there, too scared to venture off
Much too dark even for a moth
As she sat there waiting starting to dose off
Thoughts of her life before and kisses with her boss
For she was 35 alone and living in the smoke
But just six months earlier she was living with her bloke
P A for a banker she just landed her dream job
Only to find out she would be the loser and what a fucking knob
Pencil skirts hold ups and high heel
Driven to work in his expensive Italian wheels
Only looking forwards took her eye off her prize
As her new boss couldn't keep his hand off her thins
He promised her the world but she could see no truth in his eyes
First night in ages home before nine
A message on the fridge started, "Hope you're doing fine."
Then she read on
Sorry but I've left I don't think I'm the one
See darling when I meet you I wanted you so bad
But for weeks now I've try to hold your hand and talk but it only made you mad

I can't stand and think to shout back at you...you're the woman of my dreams
So I thought it best I go...cos I can't handle listen to all your screams
You finally broke me though
What you didn't know
Was when you texted me last night to say you were working late
I was with Kev...you know, you call him my fucking stupid mate
We watched you climb out of his car, smile and kiss his lips
Then held his hand and walked into that bar
I could not stand and watch you anymore
So Kev said, "Brov get in there and even up the score."
I looked in to his eye shook my disbelieving head
Jumped into a taxi and came home here instead
I lay on our unmade sacred bed
Puffed the pillows up and cried you out of my hopelessly loved up head
You got home some time just after four
heard you take your shoes off quietly closed our door
Well I could have had it out with you
But what was I going to say or do
I'm just a barman who was so in love with you
He is a banker you know I can't compete
You know I'm not for money...you are and now your complete.
So I am gone all the best
Just one last thing your boss is like the rest did you know
Just last week he was out with two other girls that are singing in a show
You're not in some exclusive club
So good luck have fun before you get the
Shove
And you were my one and only love.

You're My Tin of Sweets

Sometimes you're a toffee
Hard but sweet to shut me up when I'm a fool
Then times you're a coffee cream
Soft inside when really all you want to do is scream
Or the big purple one
I have to nibble though
To realise the nutty you
Sometimes when you're low cos me you'd like to smack
You're the triangle hard to unwrap but suck you slow you will crack
When we go to bed with lights down low
Then it's my favourite that you will show
You're the strawberry cream
Fruity, feisty Sticky and creamy
and so very steamy
With your dark and smooth outer shell
Just for me no other I would tell
You are the quality girl on our street
Thank the lord that we did meet.

Solomon Browne

Solomon Browne launched with its crew
Greenhaugh, Smith, Madron, Blewett, Brookman, Torrie and
22 year old Wallis all without a frown
Aboard their beloved Soloman Browne
Into screaming lightless unforgiving sea
For their courage was the key
Why would they go out on such a foreboding winter's night?
…where angles hid beneath their wings in fright
Trevelyan Richards at the helm
They left the safety of a cosy fire or friendly bar
Outward bound for the stricken Union Star
Out to do their lonely task saving soles without an ask
Out they steam in 50 foot waves
In their 48 foot wooden boat
Was all they had to keep the keep afloat
Trevelyan's Seamanship and a courageous crew was all they
had on this unforgiving trip
Volunteers all, no need of the whip never for bounty or favour
did they set sail
Even in this howling gale
Only one thing in their mind:
Duty to save others of their human kind
Helicopter lights guided Trevelyan though this miserable
night
…onward to his final fight
Fight they did against that bitch of a sea with all of her might
Smashing and bashing she did do never stopping
Trevelyan and his crew they did not bend: upright and strong;
grapples in hand they came along
Saved four but still there where two

Trevelyan he knew what to do
Trevelyan staunch he would stand,…was the not for port and safety of land
For a life time of 'what if's' so wheel in hand
Turned Solomon around
and again union star bound
To save them two souls before she did ground.
But alas they fought to the end
And the sea she claim all those poor souls
But they steamed into heaven without a frown
…on the bleakest of nights aboard the Solomon Browne.
For them mothers, Fathers, Sisters and Brothers Christmas will never be the same
For the sea that ran though their every vein
You're so callous now forever bow your head in shame
Now let's take a moment of our time to think hard of all the life boats and crew
…Seamen who know just what to do
Who never blink…and go to sea to save lives from ships that sink.

Surfer

There's a boy down Broad haven way
Surfs nearly every day
In summer's heat and winter's gale
In the coldest seas without fail
Humble and honest is his way to surf
Is the best in wale's here it's his turf
Not a big talker
For he says it all in that unforgiving water
He is not the biggest of men
But he is brave scores ten out of ten
The heart of a lions and lungs of a whale
29 in the world far from the end of this man's tale.
Top man Seth Morris

Where Has It Gone, Community?

Why do we have to have old people's homes
Why don't we look after the folks that looked after us, not bundled them into the kennels of death
Where them poor Mams and Dads take their final lonely breath
I'm not saying that some need the care
But would our parents have done it put theirs there
I think that years ago, only dads off to work did go
While mums stayed home and ran the family show
Not just for her the kids but checking on the vulnerable as did her mates
They were the eyes and ears watching for their gates
Old folks on every street were known and checked on ever day
Cared for in a truly loving community way
While Kids were respectful and in our street they could safely play
Dads were bests of men
Always there and allowed to discipline them
Nan's would be the tender ones teaching in their matriarchal way
Grandpa would teach in that older, calmer, patient almost play
In 30 years we have lost this community
Driven by greed and the need for money
Mams now have to go to work
For many reasons, maybe cos she married a jerk
But I feel that the cost of policing our street
Social Services, Carers too

Well that costs so much, maybe it's time to keep mums home and pay you
With them at home and loving the kids
Helping others watching from behind them keen open eyelids
Nan's and grandpa would love to help
So why did them men in power take their pensions and hope
Making them work longer just to cope
Some women may want to work kids not for them
But can still help and be a mother hen
That's for them it's their choice
They are strong and have a voice
But it's time to care for our young and youth
Kids with Knifes and gun are killing each other, do you need more proof
When all they need is discipline and dads and that's the truth.

Guns, Knives, Death and More

Old folks beaten in their home's what's it all for
What is it going to take
For the man in the street to stand up for our children's sake
We must stop hiding behind our doors
What is it going to take, next we will be burying mine or yours
We must walk together
In the sun or rain whatever whether
The men who sit protected at the top
Will not help with the blood that flows, just hand you that slaughterhouse mop
We must take the lead
Teach our kids and plant a different seed
Tomorrow take a walk down your street
Speak out, ask for help, sort out a place for you all to meet
Ask others to join in this cause
Take your streets back, for God's sake they are yours
Million died in two world wars
For this great and proud land
Boys killed in trench, on D Day beach and in desert sand
Looking down on us here below
Not in the sun, for we are hiding in the shadow
Cowards all we will not stand
Meek, frightened fucking sheep
Too scared to sort the chaff from the wheat
Just lambs…all we do is follow and bloody bleat.

Autumn

Cooling Breeze starts to whisper seductively undressing dancing trees
Chilling chimney smoke tastes in crisping air
Cattle's winter coats growing longer on their backs thickened tufts here and there
Rutting stags bellowing loud carried far in morning mist
Squirrel as he stores his nuts, in his memory he makes a list
Dormouse in his nest
Trying to sleep as they do
Hedgehog curled up trying too
Under that shed not too far from you
Egg filled lady salmon waiting in deep pools
As do their gentlemen
They're no fools
Soon to move up stream
To dance and jive laying eggs in moonlit gleam
Foxes soon start to howl
All watched by wise old owl
With shortening days
They go back to full on hunting ways
Soon winters freezing blast will again come from the east
Let only hope it does not release its beast
Or keeps it on a tight lead at least.

Brexit

We are British that's who we are
So why are we being led by people from afar
We do not owe Europe anything we sorted out your war
No thanks…not that we need it for all those men that died
Rotting in them war graves eyes now open wide
To stare in disbelief at what we have become
As we on our arses sit mute, deaf and dumb
Really we still have a vote
Them that govern are useless spineless on that you may quote
They only want to dived us as dived we shall fall
Together we should stand all for one and one for all
For now is the darkest hour we need a rallying call
A Churchill or a Thatcher not the fools that want to rule
We need a calming figure, strong that will stand up to the end
Cos right now we haven't got an EU friend
So why would we want them they lost 2 world wars
They are so fickle are they trying to even the scores
Not with bullet or bombs this time
Just a siege, stopping us trading from Britain's unique
industrial shores
Well now I tell you friends and this is how it's to be
Get ready for war and anarchy
All have the answers but none want to lead there all a bunch
of privileged poshed up chancers
None stand firm they bleat and quit not one descent fellow
They are ploughing our great country so fucking shallow
Soon it will be broken and left fallow.

Man-Made Hell

Why do folks when they have it all
Deliberately smash it up, down to them, their call
But do they realise what they do
The loved ones broken
and smashed because of you
All left to clean up the mess
But never your fault, "ah bless"
Cos you where sad and lonely misunderstood let me guess
Empty promises you made
Whilst hiding in your pardoning shade
I did not see it coming
While you were busy
lying your so fucking cunning
Well who is laughing now
You're lost and lonely in your flat
And really I'm not sorry about that
Your kids have lost their full time mother or father cos you're
a selfish prat
Just one last lingering thought
Lesson learned you hopefully have you been taught.
With that cake that you selfishly bought
Eat it cos I'm happy and in my shell
Pray to god and hopefully you will avoid your man made hell

Really, It's Not for You

Your Life is not a constant, you change in so many ways
One year, your Miss High Power, Christie's has your gaze
Next you've a mistress to an old billionaire
Stepping out in Gucci covering the best of underwear
Next it to Nice with your round the world yachtsman
Tall, dark and handsome
Then it's time to change again and trade him in
It's so easy for you like taking sweets from a Tin
Then your gaze turns west
Children and a farmer already forgot about the rest
Now this will be your hardest test
Well you tried and did you best
Cos farmers' wives are different see
They don't fail at any test
They're quiet and simply are the best
They put up with all the moaning
And god they see allot
Everyday giving family all the love they got
Feeding kids and men folk
Even when times him, she'd prefer to choke
Cos he is a rude impatient bastard sorry I meant bloke
She's up with him each morning
And watches him each night snoring in that manky old chair
While she's still bookkeeping she never thinks it unfair
She is the backbone, the wind beneath his wings
Cos let's face it lads they do so many unseen things
So lady chameleon I really enjoyed our time
But farming ain't for everyone, so good luck, farewell, go be
happy and shine.

Duel

Do you remember back in the day
When two men with issues sorted it the good old fashioned
way
When honour meant so much
When mouthy drunken louts would think before he shouts
Or tried to bully and maim
Cos back in the day he would shout up, couldn't stand the pain
Boy how things have changed respect is dead and gone
Signed away by the laws marker pen
To be never seen again
The toffs had duels and called it satisfaction
All we have now is a table and arbitration
No more can the wronged man come
knocking on the door
To even up some unjust score
Not always sorted with fists, for most a sorry was all it took
Then shake hands and turn the page
No more fighting…respect and honesty did away with all the
rage
So now it's all about lies and mouth hand bags in the bar
Bully's with Bluster and bullshit and a knife in his car
Men of substance do count anymore
And really lads that's why the army can't find enough real
men in our great country with courage to go to war.

Coppers or Officer

The job you do is very hard
That's why they give you a warrant card
It's not that you're not liked, you are, on the whole you are
the best
I very much agree that the job is not a popularity contest
But ladies and gentlemen of the force
You must be more courteous, as should we that is a must of
course
Just as you stop that car please try not to be a Sergeant major
As you're just about to bollock that young teenager, do
yourself a favour
I know you love the power trip and can't wait, licking your
lips to savour
But think again how you once were, young and dumb and full
of come
Just stop think...not your normal rule of thumb
Maybe a wry smile before you stick that nice lady on trial
Not in a sarcastic way but one that says come on love let's
sort this out and you will both be happy to go on your way
With a lesson learnt from a good bloke
Not one that all that angry way home she'd have so liked to
choke
You have the law on your side
So come on officer look let that heart open wide
Come on treat us with respect
Cos really we know your brave and are ready to protect
Just right now the trust is gone
Where once you walked, you were the respected friend of
every one
We need to sit and talk have a beer

Maybe a lock-in it won't hurt with a little cheer
Then you can become part of the community, that you so want
to do
Cos if you love us then we'll love you

Radicalisation

Radicalisation is the new word;
Do we know what it means have you heard?
Well it's to adopt radical views on political, social, issues
Think it time you reached for your box of tissues
Parents hell bent on propaganda against their ex partners
They are no better than bomb carrying wannabe suicide martyrs
Belligerently bending, beautify young sponge minds
Innocent, ignorant, impotent, impressionable that you so blend and knead
The sour lapped up with the sweet blind unconditional love this your poisoning recipe you piously feed
Your controlling low esteem, walls of guilt built from, spites and scorns
Why do you shuffle on your chequered board using kids as your pawn
Have you forgotten the child you bore with love…sent from god himself in heaven up above
Instead day and lonely night
yours is the need for this senseless spite filled fight
Think of the children and their plight
Just for once stop and think and do it right.

Woman

To the woman that stands with me
Fuck you need a medal JP
The shit that comes flowing sometimes it so deep it covers my
welly right up to my knee
But you keep me going and make me laugh
I'm hooked on you like the salmon to the poachers' gaff
They say surround yourself with them that are like you
And lady that me and you
I'm your foot and you're my shoe
This year has been one I was ready to forget
Then just as the sun was about to set
In a roundabout way we suddenly met
Each day goes flying by
Three month have passed in the blink of an eye
I never thought I'd find my match
Never for a minute find my perfect catch
But really lady you are the pill that's eased my pain
Bought me back from the darkness into the light again
Now them that know me well I can here you saying FFS what
the hell
Well Guys I'm happy cos JP has got me under her loving
spell.

My Mum

Joanie is her name now some may know of her fame
A lioness she carries no shame
Protective of her cubs
and their cubs too
Stick this family together for she is our superglue
In all the drama and god knows there have been a few
She stands strong and firm and never steps away
Even the worst that is thrown at her, even an angel would turn away
Cos being married to my dad and having me and my brother is hard enough each day
Through in the other shit she deals with as well
Really it would give an aspirin a head ache…you know, I can tell
She is always loving never mean
Her only vice is she keeps her home to clean
The grand kids want for nothing and they love her to the sky
Cos Joanie is the apple of their loving thought filled eye
Talbenny is her den and is always filled with folk
Lords and ladies rich and poor
They're all the same to Joanie and all come marching though her always open door
Some say that Joanie is dangerous and should never be allowed a pen
Well I will let you into a secret she cannot use one why would she this special mother hen
Mind careful don't upset her cubs or pride
Cos like every mother lion she can roar and bite, there will be nowhere to hide
She is loved by all that have ever crossed her path

Dotty dizzy Joanie we love you even with your farts
So shine on and don't worry you will always be so many's
Queen of Hearts

Llangwm Way

I know a man down Llangwm way
Who milks cows with his boys every single day
They are not like others this tuff old farmer with his band of
wild brothers
See they've been bought up the old fashioned way
They're workers one and all and to the farm they are hefted
and always want stay
Cos farm boys are different they don't follow like the sheep
They are proud of what they do and don't think to ever bleat
and from the youngest age are woken from their sleep
To toil with a fork in hand to move that stinking shit
Building strength, dog and grit
That's why they're the backbone of Llangwm RFC
See if not on the farm it's pill parks they will be
Dan is the eldest tallest of the lot
You will find him Saturday night dancing giving it all he's got
Aled is the scraper not a backward step he will take
Most like his father who even now in a fight is the one you
would want as your mate
Then to the youngest Carwyn
more of a lover
And like the ram the pretty ladies he loves to cover.
So to the boys from Llangwm farm hefted to their lands
Feeding this great country cos they love
to work hard with their strong calloused
hands.

Old Folks

Our country was built by the old
In times of war they stood strong never thought to fold
When Hitler came banging on Poland door
They stood their ground and went to war
As other country's through in the towel
They did not cry and sit and howl
They rolled their sleeves up and dug in
Never thinking they would not win
Not for them to think to lose that would be a downright sin
Even before the yanks joined in
Oh how we have forgot what we once were
Most young minds are addled and a blur
Well how is it to be
How are they to learn, if war came again to keep our Great
Britain, free
Cos right now from where I'm looking, see
They are meek and far too mild
It would be men fighting child
They are more interested in video games drugs and shit
And that's the good ones isn't it?
The bad ones and there are far too many running wild
No father or discipline as a child
and more are in the cue
Who is going to sort it me or you?
The stand backers give all the bullshit reasons why they are
that way
They can't sort it though and in the end we will pay
You see the kids don't start off bad on that first birthday
Cos it's learned in the home
Parents give them time put down your fucking phone

Teach them right from wrong
really do it…let's build a better country if won't take long.
You see they look and learn from you
Copying the good and bad you do
And others around them too
So sort out your mates and man or woman
Get some that are good for your kids and teach them right
It should not be a brawl and fight
And when they need discipline
Do it… Rein them in;
cos soon enough you will win
Kids are not your mate
They are our future and you they will emulate.

There Is a Man I Know

In Hartford town he was a legend and for no man he gave a
toss
Not a bully but never cross him no matter what your size and
shape he was the boss
With shovels for hands and knuckles of steel, strength of an
ape but heart on a lion
If you were daft enough to take him on you would go home
crying
but he would thank you for trying
The thing was he wasn't that tall
That's why some wanted to try him and stupidly outside they
would call
Me and him grew up see, and this is what he was taught and
told by his family day and night
It's not the dog in the fight
It's the fight in the dog
And boy in this guy they really got it right
So many tried to test him and all came unstuck
Cos he really didn't give a flying fuck
Bikers, boxers, brawlers, soldiers, police dogs and sailors
In back bar rooms, car parks, ever barns full of bailers
Sometimes for pride sometimes for money or just for fun
But never would he turn and run
But not many know the man behind the hands
Cos he was no fool and built a house all in his head never need
of any plans
He is also a talented fish man and catches them with his big
bare hands
No need for rod and line
And back then I think it was a crime

As boys I would follow and watch all a gas
As he would catch salmon trout and bass
Now his name I've not mentioned cos I'd like to see if you
know, the man of I speak of, come on have a go.

What Is a Lady?

It's a title given by Queens and Kings
But I think it means so many things
Now lads we all have our own idea of what it means
Is it because she looks after you and the kids cooks and cleans?
Or girls do you think its Gucci gown, hair styles and Jimmy Choo for your shoe?
Well I think it's a woman that can keep her head
When life is shit and all she wants to is lay in bed
Even as that tear she so longs to shed
She pushes on through all the daily crap instead
Even when the kids are screaming and fighting as she cooks tea
While her man is moaning about all the bills she can keep her calm that's her key
Till they have gone to bed then she sits him down
Puts him right in a loving way…guys you know the one where you were a fucking clown
A lady never totally loses her shit
Even when she should, when we are a total git
Even when we push our luck
Working on for that extra buck
That one last pushing it pint
As you are drunkenly realising your impending plight
When you should realise you have a lady who can fight
She can put up with our mothers
Fuck she even gets her flowers
To sum it up the Stodds way
Men You May think you're the head but your lady is the neck and the neck will always turn the head

She is the light in our everyday
She is the one that calms us in the respectful loving way
She is matriarch and this real lady is here to stay

Gelly

As a boy I watched him run and play
Scrum half for Hartford RFC he dive passed the old fashioned way
To Billy the boot he would pass
Then to the big school I did go and soon I was his pain in the ass
He had the answer to this pain and stuck me out on shoals hook grass
With that oval ball he taught boys to be men
Mostly guiding with a smile a really lovely chap
But don't be fooled if you were a dick he had his dap
Never in a wicked way and it's gone why? It should stay
This man taught kids in a special way
Boys into men he did make
Even now and I know him well I have to stop myself calling him sir
Cos respect for this man don't leave you see
Some kids that were worse than me
This man gave them time and round off their edges and mutiny
Some are now pillars of our community
This guy was not just a teacher to so many lads but their compass steering them to better things
Long after that final school bell rings.

The Zoo I Find Myself in

You're the wolf in sheep's clothing
That's opened this can of worms with your loathing
Your shaggy dog stories and lies told of me
You're like a busy stinging bee
Crocodile tears crying trying to get your deceiving ducks in row
With your…a little birdie told me so
Well let me tell you how that has gone
You should have held your horses
To late closing the gate now they have bolted
As a child you were shown
Told always let sleeping dogs lie…leave well alone
I am not like the bull in the china shop even though I'm as mad as a hornet
Having listened to your lies and blarney sending so many on your wild goose chase
Only now you're starting to slow as the truth is quickening its pace
Well now you are found out, worked out for your cheap shots
You're the leopard that will never change its spots
You were never the pick of the litter, all bark and no bite
And what you barked is a load of shite
You made the worst of errors…you came between this dog and his bone
You boiled one too many bunnies and now your chickens have come home
Your family a nest of vipers
Your friends are of your feather as you all hatefully flock together
You tried to catch this tiger by its tail

But I will not bite I am happy as truth will always prevail.
This bear you tried to prod and poke
Is now laughing the loudest at you…you're a joke.

The Great Card Game

It's a game at cards
Neither side has a winning hand
Just bullshit and a toothless demand
Johnston, Davies and others didn't have the balls and had to stack
They left the table the bad losers they did not have a winner's knack
They were worked out by Teresa the dealer May
But right now she is struggling to find
that winning, finishing hand
3 card Bragg is the game
Britain's future is the pot to our shame
The E U are at the table
Thinking that they are in control
With their primal of aces
That is a wining hand in most cases
While may is in the bluffing chair
She is blind and her cards she can't declare
And they will have to pay to see
Just one problem she don't know what they are she can only win with 3 of 3
Fair play to her mind she is got them thinking or is she playing for time
my god it's Christmas, this must be a pantomime
Really take away the prize it's just a game
to them up there at the top they just keep taking all we got
We in the end will lose, the f…king lot
Really they are gamblers one and all
They will be ok as our Britain is about to fall
they are the bullshiiters excuses ready for when they lose

These are the word they will choose duty
Best interest for our country, for all
Really how do you know this, do you have a fucking Crystal
Ball
They know no more than you or me
Like the cards they are blind and do not see.

Christmas

It's here again over indulging eating drinking and sarcastic
Banta
Excited children waiting for a fat old Santa
Is it always been this way
Or have them marketing men got their way
Turning Christmas into their advent calendar and not our
special day
When did it all become about the spend
With the banks rubbing their high interested hands
As we all lend lend lend
Pressures placed on me and you
Really by who know who
We all try so very hard for this special day
But is it really the Christian way
As we eat, drink and are trying so very hard to be merry
Sipping on that second sweet sherry
Kids now getting bored
Presents opened and in the corner carefully stacked and stored
Heating Mothers on their 4th gin
Trying to prize the turkey out of the blasted oven tin that
earlier she had lovingly carefully placed it in
Now this dinner she so wanted to deliver for all to share
Is now her mil-stone, her festive fucking nightmare
In her mind as she lay in the Christmas Eve excited bed
She was Mary Berry in her head
Burning smells shouts and fits, the fucking turkey burned to
bits
Dad is smiling getting secretly pissed
All the while getting on mother tits
Atmosphere is building looks from mam and dad

why do they do it
Put themselves, us and other through it
This special god given day
Why do we never stop and think and pray
It not about food and drink, them man made pressures that boil us up and make us shout
That come back in February as the credit card bill land on the mat
Screams of horror as dad turns white
Thinking of his impeding plight
Realise how much mum has spent
How the fuck is he going to find the overtime to pay the rent
No it's a time to do good to help others in need
We all say this year we will do it right
Not over the top just quiet and slight
Well if I may offer a little advice, about others and their plight
Out there maybe in your street out of sight
There are folks that will be sitting in their chair
Who only have the TV for company, at which they sit and stare
Who once had others too
and would spend Christmas just like you
Only now they are gone for whatever reason
Leaving them feeling lonely especially in this festive season
So shout and swear even glare
But I bet you won't help others as you should go on go on…do it and if you dare
If your Christmas is loving for all to share
I promise you would feel a god filled glow
So come on what is stopping you, give it a go.

Life

Why when things are sent to break us
So often are the very things that mend us
The day we lost our farm
Was the day god came and held us with his loving arm
Yes that day we were bruised knocked down and on the floor
We saw all we had, a life time's work smashed and broken
We did not have the words so none where spoken
Just longing looks from teary eyes
"Then fuck it we'll just have to get on and suck it," said mam
to our surprise
They say time is a healer
It is but also if you sit and let troubles overwhelm you it is the
biggest stealer
Just sit take stock then head down and push on though
It's a game no fucker really knows what to do
The only help you got is you
But if you look as you walk along the track
You will see gods signs the only way is forward so never
never never look back
He will not take you on the quickest path
It's not that simple just follow with your rod and staff
Each map is different see
It's not the same for you and me
Hard lessons to be learnt...death and life, great times too and
if you're lucky a good husband or wife
Lesson to learn every day
So look ahead and journey on enjoying all along the way
The destination is the same for all
As long as you're good in heart to one and all
So get back up if you fall or falter

Cos god is with you by your side or watching you from his altar
Guiding you on, in his silent way
If you do need a chat
stop kneel and you can pray any time night or day
Sometimes if you're lost
He will guide you just look for the signs by the way of a cross.

Stupid Woman

I'm sorry but in my eyes it's the "Stupid" that should offend not "woman".
Cos let be honest come on
She is a woman in every way
Why would that offend
She is not been under the surgeon's knife
She hasn't had bits stuck on she is a woman and been one all her life
More importantly she is not stupid of that we can clearly see
I'm no fan of Corbin and his views but they are his just not for me
The object of the row is being lost in joining the two word woman and stupid but I can't see how
If he had called her a stupid fucker
Then I think that would not be a lie
And please give me time to tell you why
She is a woman married too they must fuck
Well that's if hubby is in luck
Ladies have you ever said to your boss you stupid man
Did he take it as a gender slur, did he cry
No he didn't can you explain why
Well if I may, I will try
You see somewhere in the past you listened to words convincing you that men only wanted to control you do you really think being a woman was a sin
Your must raise up find the strength from deep down within
What is it that you found?
We don't want to keep you down on the ground
You see you don't have to keep shouting of your struggle...stop take a breath, look around

It's your time to shine Really woman in man's eyes you are quite fine
Stop playing the gender card we know you work as do we so very hard
There are going to be rows as it's been since Adam and Eve
So don't get up and shout and leave
Cos some man has called you stupid
Prove him wrong woman
No need for him to apologise
It's his opinion like an arsehole…we all got um no surprise
Stand firm do not bend
Let's sort things out time to mend
It's not a game, no one's keeping score
So woman up and stop this gender war.

Animals Are Just That

Animals are just that…they are not like you or me
Really they are not human see
Just cos Disney gave them names and a human's voice in his cartoons
For kids to watch…so why don't you see that you're not Looney tunes
It must have been your parents that forgot to tell you that animals don't love like us
They don't really go to school or work on a yellow bus
Mickey and Mini are not real, don't you see?…really aren't you able?
Did Walt draw them shitting in your cupboards or chewing your electric cable
Roland rat is a puppet voiced by a man
Now I feel it's time to tell you if I can
Truly what they are, if I may please
Rats and mice are vermin wild animals which are harmful to crops, farm animals, and carry deadly disease
That's a quote from the dictionary
Sorry if you thought they were something else to the contrary
Now you love your dog as do I
Really do you think he has human emotions, have you seen a tear, laugh, does he sit and wave bye bye
Or your cat you love so much
As he thinks to kill that tit
Do you sit him down and tell him sternly…hang on a bit
Does he listen with a grin
Then goes back to his chair and tells you how you're right and he will stay in

Does he hell…cos he is an animal we have taught him all his
tricks, taken him in from the wild
They are not, nor ever will be your adopted child
They were our vermin killers
Bred by us to do a job
Not paid in pence or bob
Yes maybe in their domesticated way they like you
As you are the Alfa and give them food to chew
It's the same for every animal…fond of them in a special way
But you must remember they were wild back in the day
So if you have love to spare
Give it to folks…that understand you and love to share

This Is My Christmas Card

Christmas is a time to forgive others
So come on sisters and brothers, have you held out that olive
branch of forgiveness
I know as god is my witness
It helps to forgive and forget
I bet still in darkened dreams you have met
Or are you still chewing on your lip
For fuck's sake get a Christmas grip
Time to do away with all this pride filled shit
Does it really matter who was right or wrong
Cos surely folks it's time to sing that different, Christmas
forgiving song
Remember back before the feud when together you were
mates
You cared about one another
Friends, lovers, sisters, brothers, father or loving mothers
When together you would laugh and kiss
hug and when not around lovingly miss
Well what went wrong?
For you to sing a different pissed off song
They ran to another's heart, after you loved them for so very
long
You both stood your ground and would not move
Both too stubborn to get back into the friendship groove
Harshly spoken word that you did not pull back
That opened up a festering puss filled growing crack
Or was it the temper that you could not control
The knee trembling punch that was thrown, landing you in
this deep dark hole
Well now it's time to search your sole

Whether the wronger or the wronged it's for you to see
Time is passing stealing your life from you
Them that you want so to make peace with, may do too
It's not a game you're not kids any more, sometimes it's the
brave that can end a war
It's the fools that let tempered pride, slam the door
So having read my Christmas card
As you sip on your Baileys and ice
Think to times long ago when everything was nice
You danced and laughed and both so very happy and daft
Why when you loved them so
How stupid it was to let them go
Or why you acted as you did flying off you fucking lid
Or are you really happy to have got rid
In this festive season
Pick up that phone and sort it out for whatever loving reason
So now please open them forgiving eyes and see
My love to you all wherever you may be.
On god's most important day
let's try to start doing thing in a more caring way.

Winter

It's here turning autumn damp and windy page
Frost and snow now fill short darkening days
Foxes scream carry's
In cold crisp crystal night
Sounding to a mate
all the while rabbits take flight
Over looked by star filled Christmas tree light sky
Duck skating on frozen ponds falling as they try
Children trying to sleep, excited in their beds
Santa's on his way
In his reindeer pulled present fill magical slay
Turkey crackling in burning stove
Spuds, sprouts, Swedes, simmer in the saucepan, as sun starts
to stare squinting, it's winter…so no full on glare
Children stirring in their bed
Soon down the wooden hills they will tread
To open presents full of Christmas cheer
Happy Christmas to all…now go have a well-earned beer.

New Year

As the new year beckons with it ageing finger
As thoughts of the year gone by still linger
The mistakes made now start to be stacked in the minds shade
Looking forward to a new year full of peace...in a sun filled glade
The friends and loved ones taken from life's path into god grace
Off to new adventures in a much better place
For us left to run this earthly...sometimes unforgiving race
With new trials and tribulations to face
Are we strong enough to keep the pace
Well with friends and loved ones still around, to do gods work, we must try of that we are duty bound
To carry on in a good and Christian way
Trying to help others every day
Not for fame or fortune, pounds or pence
Time to get off the self-righteous fence
Helping others with all our might
Shouting not whispering for what you know is right
Do not leave it to others when you know it's all our fight
Next year do not be a slacker
Step forward
not that stand backer
Think before you open your mouth...saying nothing better that Than a bullshitter
But most of all don't be a regretter
Say it...do it...you know you will feel better

You

You are the anchor that keeps my feet firmly on the ground
You are the note in my voice that make…my life so sound
You are the arms that I feel so safe in when you hold me tightly…as you wrap them around
You are the peace that I so longed for and thank god every day I found
You are the light that
Shines so bright…in every darn gone way
You are the play that makes me smile even in my darkest day
You are my breath that every minute saves me from that lonely certain death
Most of all you are my lover my soul mate…every time I see you…we are on our first date.

If This Is You... Change, Just Be Honest and Do It

Time to learn
Alone and lonely full of envy
You are your own enemy
Your choice got you there
Money over kids
Folks of power rather than folks of substance
Your mad cos your alone middle aged and so enraged
Trouble...drink is your only mate
Your history will not bring you a date
And never will you find a soul mate
Cos you need a sole of your own...you sold that long ago
Money dug your grave, like you, so shallow
You still have time to plough your life
You choose seed or fallow
Instead of treating others like shit on your shoe
Telling them where they go wrong well think it's time you really need to look at your song
Whatever it was...way back when that turned your heart into stone
Made you bad right down to your bone
It's not for me to put you right
I once tried and failed but I gave it all my might
So you must run your own race
Any friendship I once thought I could give is gone far away without any trace
For it's my own race I must run and right now I'm in first place
With another who has my pace
That loves me with a wonderful grace.

Wrangler of the Untruths

Your Bronking lies bucking and kicking
I Bloody, bruised and battered
but far from finished or shattered
Saddle sore
Hand's blistered and a little raw
I will never fail, and stay face down on the floor
As I climb back up toe in the stirrup, reins in hands, as I await
the next ride
God is here with me standing firm at my side
Waiting here in the peace filled pen
Calm, still, gentle, quite moments…
before you open the gate again
To bronk and buck back and forth sideway dipping
As I dig in my truthful spurs glistening…
trembling hands gripping
Thrown back and forth, why is no one listening
I hang on, no bell or horn does sound
From them who hide from the truths watching all around
The judges sit ring side
You're the wise…why do you not see with your eyes open
wide
As I ride bucked sitting astride these wild untamed unfounded
lies
Until the day the bell will ring, and your lying bucking is
found out
Then I will dismount throw my hat in the air and hold my
family drop to my knees and holla cry and shout.

Undertaker

Marble eyed forever watching open so very wide
Effortlessly gliding, hiding in heavens sky's
On warming thermals as they do rise
Searching, sniffing…sweet stench of death
Carried in secrecy on breeze's breath
Not for him the chase or bloody battle
Dead rotting fat and flesh is the buzzard's chattel
Once strong sheep alone…slab stone dead
Once flocked with so many here on this hill where she now
rests her head
Gorse and heather, her dying bed
As her last life filled tear here she did shed
As that undertaker glides in from his shadowless skies
Where protected he so confidently, elegantly flies
Talons grip that woollen weather proofed fleece
As the sheep has gone to graze at last found peace
Greasy lanolin does not make it easy to break the tuff tasty
skin
Then the rip…at last the buzzards in
Tearing teasing out the flesh and fat
Mutton never tasted so good as that
He fills up fast then to his paradise he must return
To soar and glide for he now has fuel to burn.

Men of the Mart

They look quite heavy as they unload, trotting in to the pen
Impartial looks from them droving men
Eight cows with calf's at foot
Dealer looks…tells me they are good "but"
There's always a "but" in the dealer's eye and I'm not going
to even ask him why…just a heavy sarcastic sigh
I turn and walk away…it's his choice to bid today
Cattle steaming in the ring
Smells of cud and sweet manure
This is the mart with its magical allure
Weather gouged features, cut from granite faces
Stick held hands that
have grappled, gripped and gone to unspeakable places
Fingers grime pitted
heads covered with hats that some loved once knitted
Stained, button missing, sting trussed tied rain coats
Hiding beneath shirts with tide stained throats
Grey old trouser lost from their jacket long ago
Left on the wet seat of tractor or under feed bags in the barrow
Standing in wellies these strong hard men of the soil
Experience learned from years of graft and toil
Once strong backs now beginning to bow
Limps and shuffles starting to show
Mind still sharp as the surgeon scalpel
Age does not bother these men, they are farmers…gods own
and what a great example
Caretakers of the land one and all
Men who may stoop but will forever stand tall.

Men

To the men that stood with me when it was kicking off all around
In front of the best supporters ever to be found
With courage, speed and grit, never thinking to submit
Men with hearts of steel…minds that could not bend
Body's that sometimes broke but they…themselves could always mend
Talkers we would meet with our shoulders we stopped them turning their talk to a breathless bleat
Sending gruff talking valley thugs back to where they came
They soon knew and spread the word about this rural county fame
We had the best of Pembrokeshire's young talent
Full of hoel never arrogant
Not one ever thought he better than his mate
Always about the team and the folks that paid on the gate
Them days I will never see again
To play with strong men that never showed their pain
Often in my dreams we meet at Lewis Lloyd ground and play and always win time and time again.

Tess

Each and every day she's there before me, hers is the winning
way
After coming first in that race
Not the front seat no
it's in the back she know her place
Barking exited can't wait to get to work
Out she gets…to the bails catching rats she know where they
lurk
Just a nip is all it takes
Then in her mouth lifeless she shakes
Drops it dead to the floor the wags her tail and look to me then
off for more
As I turn the quad key
There she is wet and muddy snuggling in to me
Eyes looking all around
What is missing and needs to be found
Off she jump nose three inches off the ground
Where has she gone I ask
Then her barks…from far off she is calling me to task
I can only here her bark
From halfway down the cliff this is not a lark
Sheep wrapped up in thorn and brambles
Chased by a leadless dog as their owner on the coastal path
disrespectfully
rambles
She guides me in with her yelp
By the pitch I can tell she needs my help
She sits patiently
So I can set her sheep free so she can guide it back thankfully
Then when that is done, by the gate she takes a pew

Waiting for me to catch up and see what is next to do
As we move through the cattle…heifer carved in the mud
I need to lift it up, watching mum as I should
For she is more dangerous than the bull
Protective with motherly hormones she is full
Then I make the biggest error take my eyes off this terror
As the heifer takes her chance…charges me and I hear its deathly bellow
I stand fear frozen to the ground and brace myself for my fate
No time for me to get to the gate
But what's that flash thank the lord it Tess
Always there for me getting me out of any mess
With a snap on the snout turned the heifer right around
Stopping her ungodly sound
I made off to the gate
Tess had saved me from my fate
Then today she showed that sly old fox she had a turn of speed
As he wandered through her flock looking for a cheeky lamb feed
She saw him run for cover
Mistake Mr. Fox now you are in serious bother
As he the hedge he tied to hop
Tess grabbed him by the scruff like the bobby this thief she did stop
He fought well but she shook him like the rat and sorry foxy that was that
Then she dragged him lifeless…dropped him dead at the gate
Then hopped into the truck, job done…now home no need to wait
And tomorrow is another day…and I know Tess will not be late

The Circle

To you that hide nameless
judging behind your desks do you really think you're blameless
Taking your shared 30 pieces of silver
Your actions…it's families you splinter
Social Services, schools, police, and most of all judges and JPs, it's not justice you deliver
Taking children from loving fathers your snakes that slither
Why do you only listen to the one sided lies
The truth is what you should find…but that's not your way. do I look surprised
Guide lines are what you hide behind
Yours is the truth to find
Let's start with the bobbies on the beat
Politicians at the top why do they're numbers…do you deplete
No time to solve a crime, no money but if they had it, would they do overtime
They are chasing lads on scooters dealing, stealing and stabbing
Why do they do this?
To quote a top judge and this is where you must take note
"They join gangs and turn to crime, as they are in need of a father figure this is provided by the gang leaders as the children crave the discipline."
Now I will go on I really hope your listening
Governments and councils make the rules for social services and schools
They are run by crooks men bent out of shape

Departments protected by their own...justice they often escape
And when they are proved to get thing wrong...a sorry no punishment the same old corrupt out of tune song
Now I come next to schools
The liberal law makes with the snowflake rules
Took away teachers cane which was used to discipline the bad and unruly fools
The school's answers now is to blame the parents and family
Well that is true I do agree
Now we are full circle if you can but see
Cos courts and lawmakers took the fathers away from their kids and his family...and we need to sort this out you and me.

North Wind

When that bully comes charging in
From the arctic with its frozen grin
stabbing, cutting at South and west
While east has gone for a rest
Trees huddle...naked no leaves to cover their shames
Farm house alone on the hill shivering windows chattering in
their frames
Sheep in the strong old barn take cover flocking
together in that golden straw
Pigs in the sty fast asleep dreaming as they snore
Cattle...frost coats their steaming backs, sticking their heads
into hedges cracks
As sly old fox passes with a crawl and stoop
Just to check if all the chicken are in the coop
Farmer sat in his chair as that fire gives off it warmth and glare
His wife tucking up the children, story told
Pillows to snuggle, warming water bottles to hold
Then farmer and wife off to bed...emmm
Good night all enough said.

New Life

I see miracles every day
Life beginning, god's special way
Lambs slowly wobble to the feet, falling down, up again they
do not fail…what grit
Then on that first journey to find that tit
How do they know where it is and what to do
Mum can't speak to give a clue
And in a field where scores are to be found
Ewe knows the sound and smell of her own
How is that she was never shown
She will stand her ground as fox or badger come to call
For her lamb she gives her all
The hen that lays her eggs then sits and incubates
Not moving only to turn them eggs for her chicks she does
patiently wait
When did she hatch this plan
Not like she watched her gran
I want to bring you parents back in from the cold
To stand up and be strong, stop being told
By them that do not have a clue
Forever telling us what to do
You bring your kids up in your own way
Full of love, happiness and play
Tell them do-gooders, to go away
Cos like the hen and ewe really you have it already in
you…and know just what to do.

To a Grown Man

Yes you are grown man tall and handsome and strong
So where is it that I went so very wrong
I'm your loving mother that's what I'll always be
See ever since you father left you your brother and me
My heart was split in three
I rolled up my sleeves and worked day and night
And I still bought you both up right
Yes there were tears and the odd fight
So why don't you call me and disappeared out of sight
We were once so very close and you always so very kind
You see son every day you're the first thing on my mind
And as I try to sleep the reasons I try so hard to find
Why have you let that woman break then take away your mind
I've tried so very hard
to deal with her in a fair a pleasant way
But really I'm stuck…why she is so very mean
Really all I'm trying to say in my loving motherly way
I love you son and miss you more and more each past and lost
day

The Boxing Match

Windswept cliffs is where I spend my day
Watch lambs as they spring and frolic they love to play
All against the grey white horse tipped waves
Roiling in lining up in a military row falling dead on rocky graves
Clouds move at a brisk pace pushed by a howling breeze
Sky and land it's the wild sea they squeeze
Fishing boats, tugs tankers too
Foam tailed tadpoles they push on though
Bring food and fuel to me and you
Buoys bobbing ducking diving punch drunk boxed out by the sea's relentless blows
Sea birds rested and left their mark white tipped where rust grows
Cliffs speckled and damp marked and gouged by that sea the champ
Even the hard granite contender strong tall and slender
Is no match for the sea with its hammer blows…and over time drops the pretender
This is where I long to be ringside at this match
Watching the sea slowly pounding taking away my patch.

House Clearance

Another grey and drizzled morn
As we make our way over this unkempt over grown once tidy
lawn
In we go Kev and me into this cold once tidy…semi
The glass pained door…lays eerily still there smashed on the
herring bone floor
The stained sofa where he lay
Three days he…alone was left to pray
Tea still in his cup he went quick no time to sup
I start to think and smell his sent
Pipe smoked by the fire
Where do we start to clear, as I find myself rolling up the telly
wire
Kev starts up stairs
Clothes in bags jackets, shirts and socks in pairs
Reg was his name or so it said on the picture in the frame
Reginald James Franklin featherweight boxing champion
Another on the wall Royal Marine commandos 1943
This is now getting personal between Reg and me
I start to glimpse into his life
Then the wedding picture he had a wife
No kids though well not in the albums just Reg and Mary
Why am I looking?
Why is his ghosts not scary?
I box up the photos no one left to give them too
Along with letters from Mary all signed with an I love you
Sent to her warrior at front
Then in the opposite draw letters from Reg
Sent in times of war
Some 70 odd years before

Blacked out word from the censers pen
But still the pain and worries of near death sounding out in all
of them
I place them carefully in the box not sure why they have no
value
Then under the stair in a locked old suit case
Kev thinks it's money and this Reg's hiding place
Screw driver in hand Kev like a safe cracker in some
Hollywood film opens it
Then throws it to me "just a load of army shit"
See Kev is not like me he is here for the cash
In his eyes if it's not money then it's trash
Well it wasn't to me it was his discharge papers and my god
Reg was the boss
And in a brown paper bag, left hidden and out of site was that
cannon smelted Victoria Cross
Given In war…fighting and killing and that where it was left
See along with the paper he had left a note
This is what it said
It's Reg that I quote
"Whoever is reading this I must be dead and gone
Read my papers the brass say I shone
That's for them and not for me
I lost many mates you see
I locked this case when I got out
And put this note in when Mary died I really I wanted to cry
and shout
I loved Mary with all my heart she saved me so many times
in all that blood and gore that is called WAR
With her 'I love yous'
The nightmares stopped when I locked the case
But came back when she left taken in god's grace
You see nothing can help as my Mary I can never replace."
So when we cleared the house and swept the glass up off the
herring bone floor
Turned the key and locked Reg's door
I took the box and case back home with me and placed them
lovingly under my stairs

See Reg cannot ever be forgotten it's not just his story but all his nightmares.

Why Do We Stand Back?

When that Lout is shouting at the lady on the till
Laughing getting his wicked thrill
Or them lads smoking swearing late at night
Or that dealer in the street you must say it…it's your right
But we don't we pass the buck
Is it really we don't give a fuck
Late in night in A+E with cans of booze shouting being mean
We all sit there heads down like we haven't seen
Bully's that we fear full of coke, booze and other gear
When did it all go so bad
I will tell…when we stopped teachers and parents from disciplining that spite full lad
Really why should we bite our lip
FFS let's get a grip
And put an end to all this shit
And let the parents, police and teachers too
Give them little bastards
their size ten shoe
Or a good hard clip
Cos mark my word if we don't do it now
There will nobody left to show you or them how.

It Is Never Too Late

The path that I was walking on
The lost, lonely, loveless one
The solitary, unfulfilling day's...dragging, dungeon dark,
drilling the sole out of me
Destination death no one to hold my dirt pitted calloused
farmed out hand as angels hover above to set my humbled
heart free
As I stumbled you caught me by the arm
Then joined me on my path, I felt safe, your agricultural ways
and cultivated charm
Smiles and laughter's, your stories of your lives' disasters
Then it happen not sure when it did begin
I fell...deep in to your beautiful big brown belonging eyes and
your never ending cheeky grin
You turned me as others went left and showed me how to go
right
You held my hand lovingly and so very tight
And walked me through that deep, dark, dread filled, night
Onwards showing me that life can be great
Thank you God, for in JP, you have given me the best ever
play(sole)mate.
So to my single friends never give up cos it's never too late.

Life

Lambs and mothers laying in the shed
Golden straw their quilted bed
Is where she, this soon-to-be mother lays her head
Lambs and ewes calling around
As her first newborn lamb hits the ground
She stands and finds him laying there sneezing
spluttering, snotty amniotic fluid, out from his lung
As she carefully licks him with her loving tongue
Then he takes his first life giving long deep breath
Steam rises from his shimmering wet woolly fleece
Soon to be forever coated in that water proofing grease
Then that first telling cry
As mother and lamb looks into each other's eye
A bond that can now only be broken if one should die
Then again mother lays still cleaning gentle grunting to her
son
As number two start to come
She does the same her rule of thumb
They both start to stand
Searching for the precious life sustaining bit
That pink warm milk giving tit
And in all the mayhem of the crowd
She will not lose them and will search until they are found
I do believe they bring her all life loving joys
Her two new born baby boys

The Litter Shitter

Wondering, watching waiting, willing you to drop your litter
Militant, mercenary's marauding, mercilessly, dishing out
fines, yes and I've named him the litter Shitter
Bully boy shady privateers, slyly sneaking
stalking, our streets, Collecting coffers for the council chaps
No signs to say they are on duty
Just pouncing fining relieving you of your hard earned
cash...that's their booty
Fag butts, gum, paper and peel
These two eye pirates watching waiting yes I do not lie they
are very real
They do not care your gender, height or age
They will nab you at any stage
They show not one ounce of human compassion
Not for them their confetti tickets to ration
Never wrong and law is on their side
So if you're going to chuck it be sure to keep you perpetrating
eyes open wide
Or better still put you fag butt, gum or peel in a bin
Then look at him with a pious grin
And don't let the Litter Shitter steal your loot
And soon enough them council chaps coffer less will give
them litter Shitter's the boot.

Sponge

They soak up what they see
Mind starting to fill with things taught by you and me
They lean so much in the nest
That in later life's lessons will put them to every unforgiving test
So give them all the right important information so they can be the best
Study them…sort out any insecurities
Give them a work ethic teach them to be busy bees
Teach them to stand up for themselves and for what is right
And always try to be polite
Curb any tempers teach hitting is not the ok
Only as a last resort in the defensive way
Talk to them and let them problem solve
Stand back and watch you won't always be around for them to involve
Nor wrap them up in cotton wool
Cos without adrenaline filled fun…life would be so dull
When they fail and they will
They must have to…alone swallow that bitterest pill
Not Molly coddled at every stage
Cos when you're gone how will they ever turn that grieving page
Tuff love is not to rage
It's to stand your ground and keep you head not give in to their childish rants at any stage
I'm not saying you or I will always get right
But when they leave our protective nest on their maiden flight
We can say in honesty…we did it lovingly, fairly but most of all we did it right

Lonely and Cold

Sitting in her arm chair TV her only friend
Coal fire that hasn't warmed since her fall but she tells all she
on the mend
The kitchen could be miles away
Stuck in this prison chair long day after day
She has few visitors...no family left at home
They left long ago and are always at the end of that phone
One son in America selling shares living in a down town
penthouse apartment
The other in Africa climbing some unknown escarpment
Her daughter with her doctoring husband a hundred miles
away
But calls her loving mother every single day
She alone brave with a smile on her old and wrinkled face
Tells them not to worry but still no fire in that cold old fire
place

Privileged Power

They sit in the white hall ivory tower
Hovering, Holding, hogging all the power
Throwing us scraps hoping we will keep wagging our faithful
tail
Privileged pals grease pole climbed all scratching each other
backs
While buggering us deep…right up to their bollockless sacks
Talking in riddles never ever all the facts
They have or will ever have to worry
Their decisions will never impact them, their family or money
We are told we have a vote
Really same old parties playing same old music on that piano
that can't sound a straight honest note
All the while we have to dance to them so dated and out of
tune
Their miming speeches written by the privileged wind filled
buffoon
Pawns to the powerful gangster of the over world
Hiding, thriving, carried on our backs
Well you Forbes named billionaires and Saudi killing princes
Diamond mining, art dealing money laundering fences
Starring out from your gated castles
Using government as your chattels
You must remember we put them there and can replace
We are ready to wipe that smirk off your privileged face
We are many…you are few and our anger is gathering pace.
Without you the wind filled buffoon.
Singing our song a pitch perfect all together tune.

Contemplation

Sitting in the lambing shed sheep still and settled laying all around
Lambs sleeping fed and do not make a sound
Time to have a thoughtful silent think
Cuppa in my hand as I take a contemplating drink
Thoughts of how I got here the path that I did take
The good times and bad left behind in my wake
So many cross road and the turns I had to make
Some say Stodds you got it made
Well let me tell you in tears I have paid
Regrets there are many
Let down by people they became two a penny
Just had to let them go…lightening my load
Travelling on…so many bumps in life's unforgiving road
They only slow me…never will I stop
For I had a dream to be a farmer not to always run the tyre shop
I must tell you friends one and all
The best times I had was when I had feckall
Never knowing where the next bob was to be found
Minder, Milkman, bouncer, window cleaner, driver
I've done them all
But never did I take my eye off that farming ball
As I sit here peace, quiet, stars above glistening in the heavens sky's
Sitting freezing cold…shit up to my eyes
You city folks may look and think me very odd
But I wouldn't have it any other way cos my calling was from god.

Vegan Activists

Why don't you do your self's a huge favour
Leave us poor carnivores alone...cos we love meat and its flavour
You poor snowflakes
I'm not sure, I think you are just fakes
Marching up bulling screaming at some hardworking farmers gate
Who toils day and night to put meat on our plate
First it was the fox hunters you tried to bait
Then you fought for TB carrying Brock that sly old foxes mate
Now it's the farmer plying his time old trade
Hiding behind your woollen masks not knowing from what they are made
You see gender neutral vegan
Really you are an anarchist's hoodlum
Band wagon jumper
Woken from your lazy city slumber
You're a shoulder chipped agitator
The countryside and its folk is who you like to harass
You knotted haired, nylon clad little bastard your starting to be a pain in the ass
Looking for trouble and your 15 minutes of TV fame
But us country boys will only be too happy and will beat you at that game
I feel it's your parents fault they are to blame
They should have made you eat your meaty tea
Then you would grow to like it just like me

It Was Different in My Day

It was not played by pumped up men that lift weights in a
disciplined way
It was played by hardworking men that earned their
weekly pay
Rugby was for men…with the boys every god-given Saturday
It was to rock up for a brutal battle
Not grabs and hand bags like now they do rattle
Liniment filled air
The same bottle from which we would each share
Kit would be tipped out on the floor
Still wet from the week before
Washed by one of the wives
They were good back then they let us have our rugby lives
Only shirts in the bag shorts and socks borrowed begged and
stolen from your mates, boots still mud covered from the
week before
Laces snapped and knotted still tying them as you go out the
door
Warm up there was none, unless you changed by a radiator
and it was on
Then out to the pitch grassless and boggy
Creosote lines black as coal
Flag posts planted in an ankle breaking hole
Goalposts rusty and bent
No padding around them just set in cement
Refs were fat and did not run
Just blew the whistle for a bit of fun
But out there it could be brutal in all the humdrum
No lines man to save you from stay boot or thumb
Fights were the norm in the day

If stayed out on the wing…they say you were gay
It was with your fists the crowd paid and had come see
Never a cry, "Ref that man's just hit me."
If you dared to go down on the ball
You would be rucked by the forwards one and all
Then back to your feet…back bleeding stud tracked…but you kept smiling even if you'd been smacked
High tackles were around the neck
Shoulder charges of course…by heck
Minutes had to pass for a late tackle
Timed by the ref that man's a jackal
Bad language was not in the game
But banter and punches allowed gone now though…ahhh what a shame
Then when the whistle blew
They were your mates again, forget about the scraps that's what you do
Just singing and drinking as all stuck together like glue
Into the cold showers
Not product and gel for hours and hours
Hair still wet as your first pint went down
That's the last I remember till next morning bad head and Mrs with a frown